**Blackstone's Police Investigators' Mock Examination Paper 2021**

Pack 1

Contents

i. Acknowledgements 3
   Introduction to the Mock Examination 3
   Instructions for Completion 6

ii. Question Booklet

iii. Answer Sheet

Score Sheet

(Please note that your score for validation questions is not included on this score sheet.)

General Principles and Police Powers	A1		A2		A3		**Total** (out of 17) (= A1 + A2 + A3)	
Serious Crime and Other Offences	B1		B2		B3		**Total** (out of 21) (= B1 + B2 + B3)	
Property Offences	C1		C2		C3		**Total** (out of 15) (= C1 + C2 + C3)	
Sexual Offences	D1		D2		D3		**Total** (out of 17) (= D1 + D2 + D3)	
							Total questions right (out of 70)	

Questions right	% score	Questions right	% score	Questions right	% score	Questions right	% score	Questions right	% score
1	1.429	15	21.429	29	41.429	43	61.429	57	81.429
2	2.857	16	22.857	30	42.857	44	62.857	58	82.857
3	4.286	17	24.286	31	44.286	45	64.286	59	84.286
4	5.714	18	25.714	32	45.714	46	65.714	60	85.714
5	7.143	19	27.143	33	47.143	47	67.143	61	87.143
6	8.571	20	28.571	34	48.571	48	68.571	62	88.571
7	10	21	30	35	50	49	70	63	90
8	11.429	22	31.429	36	51.429	50	71.429	64	91.429
9	12.857	23	32.857	37	52.857	51	72.857	65	92.857
10	14.286	24	34.286	38	54.286	52	74.286	66	94.286
11	15.714	25	35.714	39	55.714	53	75.714	67	95.714
12	17.143	26	37.143	40	57.143	54	77.143	68	97.143
13	18.571	27	38.571	41	58.571	55	78.571	69	98.571
14	20	28	40	42	60	56	80	70	100

Blackstone's Police Investigators' Mock Examination Paper 2021

Marking Instructions

Lay your answer sheet next to the marking matrix as shown; you may find it useful to fold the answer sheet to do this. Starting with Question 1, compare your marked answer (in the example this is 'C') with the correct answer given on the marking matrix. If the correct answer matches your marked answer put a '1' inside the white box on the relevant row. If it does not (see Question 2) put a '0'.

Please follow these instructions carefully to ensure accuracy. Marks ('1' or '0') should only be made in the white blank boxes (which indicate the subject area a question is related to)—please do not write anything in the grey boxes.

	Question	Answer	General Principles and Police Powers	Serious Crime and Other Offences	Property Offences	Sexual Offences	Validation
1 ▢A▢ ▢B▢ ■C■ ▢D▢	1	C	1				
2 ▢A▢ ■B■ ▢C▢ ▢D▢	2	A			0		
3 ▢A▢ ■B■ ▢C▢ ▢D▢	3	B		1			
4 ▢A▢ ▢B▢ ■C■ ▢D▢	4	C				1	
5 ▢A▢ ▢B▢ ▢C▢ ■D■	5	A		0			
6 ▢A▢ ■B■ ▢C▢ ▢D▢	6	B			1		
7 ▢A▢ ▢B▢ ▢C▢ ■D■	7	D					1

When you have marked the first 30 questions, add up the total for each column (General Principles and Police Powers; Serious Crime and Other Offences; Property Offences; and Sexual Offences) and enter the totals into the boxes marked A1, B1, etc. Then transfer these totals into the corresponding box ('A1', 'B1', etc.) on the score sheet.

28	D			0		
29	B			1		
30	C					1
Totals		A1 5	B1 3	C1 4	D1 2	E1 2

General Principles and Police Powers	A1	5	A2		A3	Total (out of 17) (= A1 + A2 + A3)
Serious Crime and other offences	B1	3	B2		B3	Total (out of 21) (= B1 + B2 + B3)
Property Offences	C1	4	C2		C3	Total (out of 15) (= C1 + C2 + C3)
Sexual Offences	D1	2	D2		D3	Total (out of 17) (= D1 + D2 + D3)
						Total questions right (out of 70)

Blackstone's Police Investigators' Mock Examination Paper 2021

Question Booklet

Time Allowed—120 minutes

1. Each of the questions is followed by four possible answers, only ONE of which is correct. Choose the ONE response that you consider to be correct. On the answer sheet mark the box that corresponds to your selection. Mark your answer clearly with a — mark. The answer sheet has spaces for your answers to all questions. If you change your mind about an answer, rub out the first mark, then mark your new answer. Mark only one answer for each question.

2. You are reminded that there is no need to read the whole examination paper before beginning to select answers to the questions posed.

3. You must ensure that BEFORE the close of the examination all of your answers to the questions have been correctly entered on the answer sheet. If you leave a question unanswered for any reason, it will not receive a mark.

4. You may make any notes you wish on the question papers.

1. NELHAM has been arrested in connection with an offence of rape (a recordable offence) and is in police detention at a designated police station. WILLSDEN, the victim of the offence, has told the police that the offender scratched her left breast with his fingers, and during a medical examination of WILLSDEN it was noted that there were several deep scratch marks on her left breast. DC LEES, the officer in the case, wishes to obtain scrapings from beneath NELHAM's nails.

   Can nail scrapings be obtained from NELHAM?

   A No, not unless an officer of the rank of inspector or above gives written authorisation for the sample to be taken.
   B Yes, as long as NELHAM has not had a non-intimate sample of the same type and from the same part of the body taken in the course of the investigation by the police or such a sample was taken but it proved insufficient.
   C No, not unless the custody officer provides authorisation for the sample to be taken (this can be oral but if oral authorisation is given it must be put into writing as soon as practicable).
   D Yes, as long as NELHAM provides his written consent to the sample being obtained.

2. CONWAY is contacted by MARLOW. MARLOW asks CONWAY to look after some jewellery for him for a few days as a favour to him; MARLOW tells CONWAY he has recently purchased the jewellery and is trying to sell it but does not want his wife to find out about his purchase as they have argued about this kind of business activity. CONWAY suspects that the jewellery may be stolen as he knows MARLOW has committed burglary offences in the past but he wants to help MARLOW so says '*Yes*'. Several hours later, MARLOW drops off the jewellery and CONWAY looks after it for a few days before MARLOW returns and takes it away. As it happens, CONWAY was right to be suspicious as the jewellery is stolen property.

   Does CONWAY commit an offence of handling stolen goods contrary to s. 22 of the Theft Act 1968?

   A No, because you must know or believe the property to be stolen to commit this offence.
   B No, because he does not get paid for looking after the property in question.
   C Yes, as suspecting that property is stolen is enough to prove this offence.
   D Yes, and he would commit the offence at the moment he arranges to handle the stolen goods.

3. DIPPER is shopping in a supermarket with his son (Andrew, aged 9 years) and his daughter (Gemma, aged 12 years). Andrew and Gemma are misbehaving and DIPPER warns them several times to stop. The children ignore DIPPER and continue misbehaving. Gemma pushes Andrew into a display of boxes of chocolates, causing a number of boxes to fall to the floor. DIPPER is angry with both children and, using the flat of his open hand, he mildly smacks both children once on the back of the leg. This causes slight reddening of the skin to both children (a transient and trifling injury). This is seen by a number of other shoppers, one of whom contacts the police about the incident.

   If DIPPER were to be charged with a s. 39 battery against the children, would he be able to utilise the defence of 'lawful chastisement' in answer to such a charge?

   A No, as s. 58 of the Children Act 2004 removed the defence of lawful chastisement from parents.
   B Yes, the lawful chastisement defence would be available to DIPPER in relation to both children.
   C No, as the defence of lawful chastisement is only available to staff in schools and others acting *in loco parentis*.
   D Yes, but the lawful chastisement defence would only be available in relation to the battery committed against Gemma.

4. BUCKINGHAM meets GODING in a bar. BUCKINGHAM is attracted to GODING but she is not interested in him so he starts telling lies about his wealth. He tells GODING that he owns several companies, has a collection of sports cars and is a multi-millionaire. He then tells GODING that he will marry her if she has sexual intercourse with him. GODING believes BUCKINGHAM and, thinking that she can gain financial advantage from his wealth by marrying him, she has sexual intercourse with him. After the sexual intercourse, BUCKINGHAM tells GODING he was lying about his wealth and his promise to marry her. GODING makes a complaint of rape to the police.

   Would BUCKINGHAM be guilty of an offence of rape (contrary to s. 1 of the Sexual Offences Act 2003)?

   A Yes, because BUCKINGHAM has deceived GODING about his wealth.
   B No, BUCKINGHAM did not use or threaten violence against GODING.
   C Yes, because BUCKINGHAM made a false promise to marry GODING.
   D No, as GODING consented to sexual intercourse with BUCKINGHAM.

5. TAPSTER is using an internet chat room with DODD and ANGUS. TAPSTER has an argument with DODD and becomes so angry he writes a message "*I'm gonna kill DODD next week*" and sends it to ANGUS. TAPSTER does not intend to make ANGUS think he is going to kill DODD, he is just incredibly angry and is venting his frustration. Unfortunately, ANGUS sees the message and believes it and contacts the police; DODD never sees the message and is oblivious to its existence.

   In relation to the offence of threats to kill (contrary to s. 16 of the Offences Against the Person Act 1861), which of the following comments is correct?

   A The offence has not been committed because TAPSTER did not intend ANGUS to fear that DODD would be killed.
   B The offence has not been committed as the threat was to kill a person in the future, not there and then.
   C The offence has not been committed because the person who was to be killed was unaware of the threat.
   D The offence has not been committed because the offence cannot be committed via a third party.

6. CORRIGAN wants to make some easy money and purchases 10 fake designer handbags from a criminal associate. He intends to sell the handbags at a car-boot sale. He drives to the car-boot sale and sets up his stall. He places a sign that says 'Genuine "Mulberry" Handbags for Sale—Normally £600—Today £50.00!' on a table next to the handbags. JACKSON picks up one of the bags and asks, '*Are these the real deal, then?*' To which CORRIGAN replies '*100% genuine—they're a bargain, eh?*' JACKSON is not fooled as the bags are of such poor quality that she is not taken in and leaves the stall. In fact, CORRIGAN does not sell a single bag.

   Does CORRIGAN commit an offence of fraud by false representation (contrary to s. 2 of the Fraud Act 2006)?

   A No, CORRIGAN does not commit the offence as he did not sell any of the bags and consequently he did not gain anything from his activity.
   B Yes, the offence is committed at the moment he places the sign next to the handbags.
   C Yes, but the offence is not committed until he tells JACKSON that the handbags are '*100% genuine*'.
   D No, CORRIGAN does not commit the offence as nobody was actually deceived by his behaviour.

7. WALTON contacts the police to complain about what she thinks is large-scale drug dealing and drug use taking place outside the rear of a social club in a village location. WALTON is aware of the activity as her house is one of a number of houses located at the rear of the social club. WALTON speaks to DC FLETCHER about the activity and tells DC FLETCHER that he can use her house to watch what is going on. DC FLETCHER wishes to obtain evidence in relation to this activity by the use of a surveillance device (in this case a camera) and also from officers who will operate the camera and make notes of the activity. The camera and the officers will be located in WALTON's house.

    Thinking about the law in relation to directed and intrusive surveillance (dealt with by the Regulation of Investigatory Powers Act 2000), which of the following comments is true?

    A Such activity would be classed as directed surveillance and an authorisation for the surveillance to take place should be sought from an officer of the rank of inspector or above.
    B Such activity would be classed as intrusive surveillance and an authorisation for the surveillance to take place should be sought from an officer of the rank of superintendent or above.
    C Such activity would be classed as intrusive surveillance and an authorisation for the surveillance to take place should be sought from an officer of the rank of chief constable/commissioner (or his/her designated deputy).
    D Such activity would be classed as directed surveillance and an authorisation for the surveillance to take place should be sought from an officer of the rank of superintendent or above.

8. BEEDLE is in a pub when she is approached by KITSON, who is drinking with a group of his friends. KITSON tries to engage BEEDLE in conversation and asks if she would like a drink; BEEDLE is not interested in KITSON and politely says 'No thanks'. BEEDLE's friends roar with laughter at his rejection and, feeling humiliated and for the purposes of his sexual gratification, KITSON puts his hands on BEEDLE's breasts (over the top she is wearing) and shouts 'Well, how about a fuck then!'

    Would this constitute an offence of sexual touching (contrary to s. 3 of the Sexual Offences Act 2003)?

    A Yes, because touching includes touching through the clothing.
    B No, KITSON did not touch BEEDLE's genitals.
    C Yes, because KITSON did it for the purposes of sexual gratification.
    D No, because the touching was not with KITSON's penis.

9. HANCOCK is wanted for a serious armed robbery where he used a revolver to threaten staff. He resides in a small block of flats and a team of armed officers go to his flat in the early hours of the morning to arrest him. The officers surround the premises but, before they go up the stairs to his flat, HANCOCK appears at the top landing and fires two shots at PC FLINT, one of the armed officers. FLINT returns fire but a split second before he does HANCOCK pulls his girlfriend, SIMPSON, in front of him as a shield. The officers return fire and kill SIMPSON. HANCOCK then places his hands in the air in surrender and is formally arrested.

   Which of the following statements is correct with regards to the criminal liability of HANCOCK?

   A HANCOCK is guilty of the murder of SIMPSON.
   B HANCOCK is guilty of voluntary manslaughter of SIMPSON.
   C HANCOCK is guilty of involuntary manslaughter by unlawful act.
   D HANCOCK is not liable in these circumstances for the death of SIMPSON.

10. SHEFFIELD is attacked and robbed by TAYLOR (who is a stranger to SHEFFIELD). DC McCUBBIN is first to arrive at the scene of the offence and quickly obtains a first description of TAYLOR from SHEFFIELD. DC McCUBBIN places SHEFFIELD in an unmarked police vehicle and drives SHEFFIELD around the local area to see if he can identify the person responsible for the offence. They drive along a busy street with a cafe on one side of the road and a pub on the other. People are outside both premises and SHEFFIELD is looking intently at a group outside the cafe. DC McCUBBIN sees a person who matches the description given by SHEFFIELD standing outside the pub with a group of people and asks SHEFFIELD to look closely at the group outside the pub. As a result, SHEFFIELD identifies TAYLOR who is in the group outside the pub and is subsequently arrested by other officers searching the area.

    In relation to Code D of the Codes of Practice, which of the following comments is correct?

    A Code D has not been complied with as once a first description of an offender has been obtained from an eye-witness they should not take part in any 'street' identification process.
    B Code D has not been complied with as DC McCUBBIN is not allowed to draw the attention of SHEFFIELD to a particular group.
    C Code D has not been complied with as at least two officers must be present when such a 'street' identification process takes place.
    D Code D of the Codes of Practice has been complied with by the officer.

11. ROSS works as a clerk for a large car sales firm. She is examining a number of expenses claims (required for accounting purposes) that have been submitted by FINLAY (a supervisor at the car sales firm). ROSS discovers a significant number of irregularities suggesting that expenses amounting to £3,000 are false and she confronts FINLAY regarding the irregularities. FINLAY admits the expenses are false but threatens ROSS to the effect that if she does anything about the false claims he will make sure she loses her job, and he tells ROSS to falsify the expenses claims so that they appear genuine. FINLAY has a great deal of influence at the firm and ROSS honestly believes he could get her sacked. ROSS fears that this loss of income will have a dramatic impact on her standard of living and she falsifies the expenses for FINLAY.

    Would ROSS be able to claim that she was acting under duress of circumstances in relation to any offences that she commits by falsifying the expenses claims?

    A No, as she did not have cause to fear she that would suffer death or serious injury if she did not do as FINLAY demanded.
    B Yes, as the defence is available in answer to any charge except for treason.
    C No, as duress of circumstances is only a defence to a charge of murder or attempted murder.
    D Yes, because she honestly believed that she would be sacked if she did not do as FINLAY demanded.

12. WILSON has been arrested for drug-related crimes. At the custody block the arresting officer informs the custody sergeant that there is evidence that WILSON has swallowed some drugs. WILSON's detention is authorised and the officers wish to carry out an X-ray or ultrasound scan on WILSON.

    In order to comply with s. 55A of PACE 1984 which of the following statements is correct?

    A The drug swallowed must be a Class A drug and have been for supply or export. The authority required is that of an inspector (along with the consent of WILSON) and no force can be used.
    B The drug swallowed must be a Class A and have been for supply or export. The authority required is that of an inspector and force can be used.
    C The drug swallowed can be a Class A, B or C and have been for supply or export. The authority required is that of an inspector (along with the consent of WILSON) and no force can be used.
    D The drug swallowed can be a Class A, B or C and have been for supply or export. The authority required is that of an inspector and force can be used.

13. WEBSTER is obsessed with SMALL and thinks that she is the most beautiful woman he has ever seen. He has made sexual advances to her on numerous occasions but she has rejected him, telling him in no uncertain terms that she thinks he is a loser and that she would never want to have anything to do with him. This has made WEBSTER extremely angry and he decides that he will kidnap SMALL and humiliate her. He waits outside her house one evening and as she arrives home from work WEBSTER grabs her and bundles her into a van. In the van, he ties SMALL up, rips off her clothing and subjects her to a sexual attack. He forces a dildo into SMALL's mouth causing her to violently gag on it. He then pushes the dildo into her anus causing her to scream in pain. Finally, he pushes open her legs and forces the dildo into her vagina.

    At what stage, if at all, is the offence of assault by penetration (contrary to s. 2 of the Sexual Offences Act 2003) first committed?

    A When WEBSTER forces the dildo into SMALL's mouth.
    B When WEBSTER forces the dildo into SMALL's anus.
    C When WEBSTER forces the dildo into SMALL's vagina.
    D The offence has not been committed as WEBSTER did not use a part of his body to carry out any of the penetrative acts.

14. MORGAN goes on holiday for two weeks. While MORGAN is away, and without the permission of MORGAN, FLOYD (MORGAN's next-door neighbour) moves the garden fence that separates their respective gardens 1 metre onto MORGAN's property, thus incorporating a strip of MORGAN's land onto his estate. FLOYD then digs up and removes an entire cultivated small cypress tree (including its roots) from the strip of MORGAN's land he incorporated into his estate.

    Has FLOYD committed an offence of theft (contrary to s. 1 of the Theft Act 1968) in these circumstances?

    A Yes, but only in relation to the strip of land he incorporates into his estate.
    B No, the offence of theft has not been committed by FLOYD because the land is not 'property' and the cypress tree was not taken for sale, reward or other commercial purpose.
    C Yes, but only in relation to the cultivated cypress tree he removed from MORGAN's land.
    D No, because there are no circumstances whatsoever whereby land can be stolen.

15. BORMAN (who is 19 years old) is standing outside a newsagents which is near to a school and is regularly frequented by school pupils on their way to the school. He engages in conversation with MOORE (who is 14 years old and dressed in school uniform) and during the conversation MOORE invites BORMAN to touch her breasts. BORMAN realises that MOORE is under 16 but this does not stop him fondling MOORE's breasts. This activity is witnessed by TANSILL who is working in the newsagents. TANSILL contacts the police and PC MILNER attends the scene.

    Does BORMAN commit the offence of sexual activity with a child (contrary to s. 9 of the Sexual Offences Act 2003)?

    A No, as MOORE is over 13 years old.
    B Yes, and as MOORE is under 16 there is no requirement for the prosecution to prove anything regarding BORMAN's belief about MOORE's age.
    C No, as MOORE consented to the activity.
    D Yes, but the prosecution must show that MOORE was under 16 and that BORMAN did not reasonably believe she was 16 or over.

16. KING meets JOSSE in a pub and the two begin to chat. They get on extremely well with each other and agree to have sexual intercourse at KING's house. At KING's house, the two begin to remove their clothes, at which point JOSSE tells KING that whilst she is 100% willing to have sexual intercourse with him it will be on the strict understanding that he wears a condom during the act as she is concerned about the transmission of sexual infections. KING assures JOSSE that he will wear a condom during the act. The problem for KING is that he does not have a condom in his possession. KING takes JOSSE into his bedroom and turns all the lights out so that JOSSE cannot see what is going on. JOSSE asks KING if he is wearing a condom to which KING replies that he is. On that basis, JOSSE has full sexual intercourse with KING.

    Is KING liable for the offence of rape in these circumstances?

    A No, because JOSSE consented to the act of sexual intercourse.
    B Yes, as it is a condition of the sexual act that KING wear a condom.
    C No, as JOSSE did not contract a sexually transmitted infection.
    D Yes, and s. 76 of the Sexual Offences Act 2003 would apply as KING deceived JOSSE as to the nature of the act.

17. MINCHER and DUDLEY are old friends who used to be at university together. They meet in a pub for a reunion drink—MINCHER drinks a couple of pints of lager but DUDLEY is driving so she is only drinking lemonade. During their conversation, MINCHER reminds DUDLEY of the fun they used to have when they took drugs together and states that he has some LSD with him and asks DUDLEY if she would like some for 'old times' sake'. DUDLEY politely refuses. DUDLEY visits the toilet of the pub and while she is away, MINCHER places a 'tab' of LSD in her lemonade. He swallows some LSD himself and when DUDLEY returns from the toilet she drinks her lemonade, swallowing the LSD in the process. The drug intoxicates MINCHER and DUDLEY who both begin to behave in an extremely erratic fashion resulting in GALLON (the landlord of the pub) requiring the two to leave the premises. MINCHER and DUDLEY attack GALLON causing him actual bodily harm (s. 47 of the Offences Against the Person Act 1861). The police are called and MINCHER and DUDLEY are arrested.

    In relation to the law regarding intoxication and its use as a 'general defence', which of the following comments is correct?

    A Intoxication is only relevant when the source of the intoxication is alcohol.
    B As a s. 47 assault is a 'basic' intent offence, intoxication (whether it be from drink or drugs) would have no relevance for either of the accused.
    C As DUDLEY was involuntarily intoxicated, she would be able to raise 'intoxication' in defence to a charge of s. 47 assault.
    D It does not matter that MINCHER was voluntarily intoxicated as a result of taking the LSD—he could still raise the issue of intoxication in defence to a charge of s. 47 assault.

18. MASON and BAYTON work in the same office building and sometimes have dealings with each other in a professional capacity. As far as MASON is concerned, the two are work colleagues and nothing more. However, BAYTON thinks that MASON is in love with her and is obsessed with MASON as a result. BAYTON publishes a statement on her Facebook page telling all of her friends that she has received a letter from MASON telling her that he is in love with and wants to marry her (this is a total fabrication by BAYTON). This causes MASON some embarrassment in his workplace but nothing more as he laughs it off as a joke. The following day, BAYTON sends an email to MASON telling him that she loves him and that if she sees him with another woman she will kill herself. As a result of BAYTON's continued behaviour, MASON's performance at work deteriorates due to stress brought on by BAYTON's activities.

    Has BAYTON committed an offence of stalking (under s. 4A of the Protection from Harassment Act 1997)?

    A Yes, the offence under s. 4A has been committed by BAYTON when she publishes the statement about the love letter on her Facebook page.
    B Yes, the offence under s. 4A has been committed by BAYTON when she sends the email to MASON threatening to kill herself if she sees him with another woman and because of the consequent effect it has on MASON.
    C No, the offence under s. 4A has not been committed by BAYTON as she has not caused MASON to fear, on two occasions, that violence will be used against him.
    D No, the offence under s. 4A has not been committed because the course of conduct pursued by BAYTON does not amount to 'stalking'.

19. PCs HALL and SIMON are directed to a report of a high-value robbery at a jewellers. On arrival, the officers speak to the owner of the shop who provides them with the description of two men who have made off with at least £2 million pounds' worth of jewellery. The officers carry out an immediate search of the area and find, arrest and caution one of the men responsible, GOULD. GOULD is searched but does not have any of the stolen jewellery on his person. PC HALL asks GOULD, *'Where is the jewellery?'* to which GOULD does not respond. PC SIMON asks GOULD, *'C'mon, this isn't a couple of gold rings, this is two million quids' worth, we need to know now, where is it?'* GOULD replies, *'My mate has it, we split up after the robbery and we're supposed to meet up later on tonight at his house, the jewels will be there in about 30 minutes' time.'* GOULD then tells the officers the address of his associate.

    Which of the following comments is true in relation to the behaviour of the officers?

    A The interview is illegal as Code C of the PACE Codes of Practice states that any interview of a person under arrest must take place at a police station.

    B The officers should not have interviewed GOULD without the authorisation of an officer of at least the rank of superintendent.

    C The interview of a person under arrest should take place at a police station unless waiting to do so would lead to physical harm to people; therefore the interview of GOULD in the vehicle is not permitted in this situation.

    D The officers are acting correctly if they think any delay in interviewing GOULD could hinder the recovery of property obtained in consequence of the commission of the robbery offence.

20. PC SLATER is on patrol and is dispatched to a small wooded area where a person has reported finding an insecure shed. On arrival, PC SLATER cannot find the person who called the police but identifies the shed. On entering the shed, the officer finds several guns and rifles and other paraphernalia for supporting a terrorist group. PC SLATER immediately cordons the area under his powers under s. 34 of the Terrorism Act 2000 (by reason of urgency) for an investigation.

    Which of the following statements is correct with regard to further compliance under s. 34 and s. 35 of the Terrorism Act 2000?

    A An officer of at least the rank of superintendent is informed and if continued designation is confirmed the initial designation can be only for a maximum of 7 days.

    B An officer of at least the rank of superintendent is informed and if continued designation is confirmed the initial designation can be only for a maximum of 14 days.

    C An officer of at least the rank of ACC/Commander is informed and if continued designation is confirmed the initial designation can be only for a maximum of 7 days.

    D An officer of at least the rank of ACC/Commander is informed and if continued designation is confirmed the initial designation can be only for a maximum of 14 days.

21. POXSON has been at a house party and is walking home in the early hours of the morning as he has no money for a taxi. He is tired and decides to take a car to get him home. He picks up a brick and smashes the front driver side window of a Ford Mondeo and gets inside intending to drive off in the vehicle. He manages to start the engine of the vehicle and sits in it for a few moments before he presses the accelerator. He stalls the vehicle almost immediately so that it only moves 4 feet along the road.

    Considering the offence of taking a conveyance without consent (contrary to s. 12 of the Theft Act 1968) and the law connected to it, which of the following statements is correct?

    A The offence is complete when POXSON smashes the window of the car and gets inside intending to drive off in it.
    B The offence is complete when POXSON starts the engine of the vehicle and sits in it for a few moments.
    C The offence is complete when POXSON moves the vehicle 4 feet.
    D The small amount of movement means that the offence has not been completed and POXSON should be prosecuted for an offence of attempting to take the conveyance without consent (contrary to s. 1(1) of the Criminal Attempts Act 1981).

22. DOBBS is a well-known drug dealer and also owns a night club. He is notorious in the area for his criminal behaviour, but all prosecutions have been unsuccessful. DOBBS asks READ, a local builder, to quote him for a new roof to his garage block. READ's quote is for £4,500—a realistic price for the work—and DOBBS tells READ that he will pay in cash. READ suspects that the money is from DOBBS's drug-dealing activities, but accepts the job as his business is struggling. READ completes the work and is paid in cash and declares the full amount of this as income on his accounts. DOBBS is arrested 18 months later and a successful prosecution brought against him for drug dealing.

    Does READ commit an offence contrary to s. 329 of the Proceeds of Crime Act 2002 (acquisition, use and possession of criminal property)?

    A No, as DOBBS was arrested more than 12 months after the money was paid to READ.
    B Yes, READ is guilty of the offence as he suspected that the money came from criminal activity.
    C No, as READ received the money as adequate consideration for the work he completed.
    D Yes, because he accepted cash suspecting DOBBS's criminal activities and this assisted in its disposal.

23. Officers raid a house following intelligence that persons responsible for several burglaries in the area are residing at the address. The suspects are arrested and taken into custody. PC HALDER is placed at the gate of the front of the property because of local media interest, just inside a taped off cordon, whilst other officers search the property. After a short while a news team with cameras set up opposite the premises outside the taped off area. STONE, a brother of one of those arrested, arrives at the property and is very annoyed that his brother has been arrested. STONE approaches PC HALDER and leaning over the tape he shouts, *'You fucking pig, if these cameras weren't here, you shit, I'd beat the crap out of you!'*

    Which of the following statements is correct with regard to offences of assault only?

    A STONE commits the offence of s. 39 common assault as he intended PC HALDER to apprehend the immediate infliction of unlawful force.
    B STONE only commits the offence of attempt s. 39 common assault as there was no battery.
    C STONE commits the offence of assaulting a constable in the execution of his duty even though he used only words.
    D STONE does not commit an assault in these circumstances.

24. Henry SINCLAIR is an 18-year-old male and lives with his step-sister, Jayne RAYNOR, who is 16 years old and both their respective parents, his father and her mother; both the parents are widowed. Henry and Jayne have been step-brother and sister for the last five years. During this time they have become very close and have fallen in love; however, because of their very religious upbringing they have remained totally celibate. Henry asks Jayne to marry him and her mother gives the appropriate legal consent. They marry two weeks before Jayne's 17th birthday.

    Considering offences contrary to s. 25 of the Sexual Offences Act 2003 (Sexual Activity with Child Family Members), which of the following statements is correct?

    A Henry and Jayne cannot have sex until she is 17.
    B Henry and Jayne can have sex because they are married.
    C Henry and Jayne cannot have sex until she is 18.
    D Henry and Jayne can have sex as they are not blood relatives and she is 16 years or over.

25. SPEED is being interviewed for an offence of burglary and has answered 'no comment' to the questions asked of him. He realises that the police have a lot of evidence against him and so asks for a short break while he gathers his thoughts. As it will be a short break, no persons leave the interview room.

    To comply with Code E of PACE, which of the following statements is correct with regard to procedures to be taken for short breaks in interviews?

    A If a short break is taken then it should be treated as the end of an interview; the relevant sealing and signatures are required.
    B If a short break is taken then both the interviewer and the suspect can remain in the interview room and the recording media may be stopped; when the interview recommences the same recording media can be used.
    C If a short break is taken then both the interviewer and the suspect can remain in the interview room and the recording media must not be stopped and must remain on for the duration of the short break.
    D As this is a short break then the officers must leave the room to allow the detainee to gather their thoughts but the recording media can be switched off and when the interview recommences the same recording material can be used.

26. BUCHANAN is a British citizen who owns several holiday homes in Italy. He is visiting Naples when he sees ALI, a refugee from Libya, begging on a street. BUCHANAN approaches ALI and asks her if she is interested in working for him as a maid in one of his holiday homes a short distance away on the Amalfi Coast of Italy and tells her the job comes with food and lodging. ALI is delighted at the prospect and replies that she is interested. BUCHANAN tells her that she will need to meet him in a side street around the corner from their current location in one hour and he will drive her to the holiday home. BUCHANAN actually intends to take ALI to the house to exploit her by forcing her into prostitution. One hour later, BUCHANAN meets ALI and drives her to the holiday home. During the journey, ALI becomes suspicious of BUCHANAN and manages to escape when he stops for fuel.

    Has BUCHANAN committed an offence of human trafficking (contrary to s. 2 of the Modern Slavery Act 2015)?

    A No, as the activity (arranging ALI's travel) takes place in Naples this would not constitute an offence under s. 2 of the Act.
    B Yes, but only when BUCHANAN actually picks ALI up and drives her to his holiday home with a view to exploiting her.
    C Yes, the offence has been committed by BUCHANAN as soon as he arranged the travel of ALI with a view to her being exploited.
    D No, as BUCHANAN intended to exploit ALI outside the United Kingdom (he intended to exploit her in Naples).

27. TENANT, an adult male, is working in York for the week as a representative of a chemical company. In the bar of the hotel he engages in conversation with HANNAH, an adult female. TENANT buys HANNAH several drinks and they start becoming very tactile with each other. Unbeknown to TENANT, HANNAH is a paranoid schizophrenic (a mental condition) so when TENANT suggests they go to his room for sex HANNAH agrees solely because of her condition, believing that it is right to do so. In TENANT's bedroom they have oral sex.

    Does TENANT commit an offence of sexual activity with a mentally disordered person contrary to s. 30 of the Sexual Offences Act 2003?

    A No, TENANT has to be aware that HANNAH was suffering from a mental disorder.
    B Yes, the offence includes oral sex and there does not have to be full intercourse.
    C No, as TENANT has to have sexual intercourse with HANNAH for the offence to be complete.
    D Yes, but as TENANT was not aware of HANNAH's mental disorder it is therefore a summary only offence.

28. HENNIGAN owns a Ford Mondeo car which requires a routine service and some minor repair work. He takes it to a garage and speaks to TREMELING (the owner of the garage) and asks for the work to be carried out on the car. HENNIGAN gives the car keys and vehicle to TREMELING who give the keys and vehicle to ORCHARD who is a mechanic working at TREMELING's garage. TREMELING tells ORCHARD to carry out the work on the car. ORCHARD services and repairs the car using parts purchased by TREMELING and stored in TREMELING"s garage. ORCHARD then takes the car out for a test drive.

    At the time ORCHARD takes the car out for a test drive, who could the vehicle be said to 'belong to' for the purposes of s. 5 of the Theft Act 1968?

    A Only HENNIGAN as he is the owner of the vehicle.
    B HENNIGAN as the owner and ORCHARD as a person who has possession of the vehicle.
    C Only ORCHARD as he is the only person who has possession of the vehicle.
    D HENNIGAN as the owner, TREMELING as a person who has a proprietary interest in the car and ORCHARD who has the vehicle in his possession.

29. KNOWLE and COLLIER are drinking in a pub and discussing their sex lives. KNOWLE tells COLLIER he has not had sex for six months. COLLIER feels sorry for KNOWLE and tells him that he knows a prostitute (ORCHARD) who will have sex with KNOWLE for £100. KNOWLE tells COLLIER he does not have the money so COLLIER tells KNOWLE he will 'treat him'. They visit ORCHARD's home address and on arrival COLLIER asks to speak to ORCHARD in private. COLLIER lies to ORCHARD telling her that he has paid her 'pimp' the £100 for her to have sex with KNOWLE so there will be no need for cash to be exchanged. ORCHARD believes COLLIER and, on the basis that the sex has been paid for, she has sexual intercourse with KNOWLE. KNOWLE has no idea about what COLLIER has done.

Has an offence of obtaining services dishonestly (contrary to s. 11 of the Fraud Act 2006) been committed by COLLIER in these circumstances?

   A No, as the 'service' that has been obtained related to prostitution and prostitution is contrary to law, therefore the offence has not been committed.
   B Yes, the offence is committed at the point when COLLIER lies to ORCHARD about the money being paid to her 'pimp'.
   C No, the offence has not been committed by COLLIER as the service he obtained was not for himself.
   D Yes, the offence is committed when ORCHARD has sexual intercourse with KNOWLE.

30. PARSON (aged 19 years) shares a two-bedroom flat with CLARK (aged 17 years). PARSON pays 70% of the rent and other expenses because he earns more than CLARK; they are just flatmates. PARSON, however, believes this to be unjust and persuades CLARK that he needs some form of reward for paying the majority of the bills. PARSON persuades CLARK to masturbate him once a week as compensation; CLARK does not want to do this but complies. The owner of the flat puts up the rent and PARSON now decides that CLARK need not masturbate him anymore but will have to prostitute herself as she cannot pay any more towards the bills; she has no option but to agree to PARSON's requests. A couple of times a week CLARK performs sexual acts with other men for money.

Considering s. 4 of the Sexual Offences Act 2003 (causing a person to engage in sexual activity without consent), which of the statements below is correct?

   A PARSON only commits this offence when he forces CLARK to masturbate him.
   B PARSON does not commit any offences under s. 4 because CLARK is over the age of 16.
   C PARSON commits this offence when he forces her to masturbate him and when he forces her to prostitute herself.
   D PARSON only commits this offence when he forces her to prostitute herself.

31. Section 1 of the Child Abduction Act 1984 provides a defence whereby a person does not commit an offence under this section by taking or sending the child out of the United Kingdom without the appropriate consent if either he has a child arrangement order in force in respect of the child or he is a special guardian of the child. This defence under s. 1 of not requiring the appropriate consent has time limits for the sending or taking of the child out of the United Kingdom.

    In relation to those time limits, which of the statements below is correct?

    A Both persons with a child arrangement order and special guardians can take or send the child out of the United Kingdom without the appropriate consent for a period of less than one month.

    B Both persons with a child arrangement order and special guardians can take or send the child out of the United Kingdom without the appropriate consent for a period of less than three months.

    C Persons with a child arrangement order can take or send the child out of the United Kingdom without the appropriate consent for less than one month and special guardians for less than three months.

    D Persons with a child arrangement order can take or send the child out of the United Kingdom without the appropriate consent for less than three months and special guardians for less than one month.

32. MANNIGER is sick to death of the behaviour of SMITH who is in the habit of parking his car outside MANNIGER's house and playing his music extremely loudly and late at night causing MANNIGER to lose sleep. One evening, MANNIGER has had enough and goes out onto the street and confronts SMITH who is sitting in the driving seat of the car with his girlfriend, INCE, sitting in the front passenger seat. MANNIGER states, *'If you don't stop playing that loud music I will follow you home and pour paint stripper all over this car!'* MANNIGER intends SMITH to fear that his car will be damaged. SMITH is completely unconcerned by the threat and does not believe MANNIGER although INCE does believe the threat.

    Does MANNIGER commit the offence of threats to destroy or damage property (contrary to s. 2 of the Criminal Damage Act 1971)?

    A No, the offence has not been committed as this is a 'conditional' threat (if SMITH stops playing the music, the damage will not occur).

    B Yes, the offence has been committed as MANNIGER intends SMITH to fear his or another's property will be damaged.

    C No, the offence has not been committed as SMITH does not believe MANNIGER.

    D Yes, the offence has been committed as INCE believes that MANNIGER will carry out the threat and damage SMITH's car.

33. THOMAS has been arrested in connection with an offence of kidnapping. The victim of the kidnap, HUDSON, has not been found and there is great concern about her safety. There is sufficient evidence to provide a realistic prospect of conviction for the offence and consequently THOMAS is charged with kidnapping (contrary to common law). When THOMAS is charged with the offence and cautioned, he responds to the caution by saying, *'I want to tell you where she is'*.

    Could THOMAS be interviewed about the offence of kidnapping at this stage?

    A No, as THOMAS has been charged with the offence, he may not be interviewed any further in relation to it.
    B Yes, as the interview would take place to prevent or minimise harm to some other person.
    C No, as the person charged can only be further interviewed in order to clear up an ambiguity in a previous answer or statement.
    D Yes, as long as an officer of the rank of superintendent or above authorises the interview to take place.

34. DC FAYED is working in the Criminal Investigation Department at his station when he receives good-quality intelligence from a trusted source in relation to the location of a large amount of stolen goods. The stolen property is alleged to be located at five different premises and after briefly discussing the matter with his supervisor, DC FAYED decides to make an application to search all the premises (an 'all premises' warrant). Due to the nature of the intelligence received by DC FAYED, he decides to request that the warrant allow entry to the target premises on multiple occasions.

    In relation to the procedures under ss. 15 and 16 of the Police and Criminal Evidence Act 1984 (application for a warrant and execution of a warrant) and Code B of the Codes of Practice, which of the following comments is correct?

    A Applications for multiple premises and multiple entry warrants must be made with the written authority of an officer of at least the rank of superintendent (although in urgent cases where a superintendent is not readily available, the most senior officer on duty may authorise the application).
    B Entry and search under such a warrant must be made within one month from the date of its issue.
    C No premises may be entered or searched for the second or any subsequent time under a warrant which authorises multiple entries unless a police officer of at least the rank of inspector has, in writing, authorised that entry to those premises.
    D If the warrant is an all premises warrant, no premises which are not specified in it may be entered and searched unless a police officer of at least the rank of superintendent has, in writing, authorised them to be entered.

35. WASHINGTON and DRISCOLL have an argument in a pub resulting in WASHINGTON threatening to give DRISCOLL a *'good old-fashioned black eye!'* DRISCOLL is frightened by WASHINGTON's threats and runs out of the pub and gets into his car to get away from the pub as fast as he can. He is inside his car when he sees WASHINGTON run out of the pub and towards him. DRISCOLL feels that he is going to be assaulted by WASHINGTON and so starts his car and drives towards WASHINGTON, hitting him and throwing him over the bonnet of the car and causing WASHINGTON serious physical injury. DRISCOLL is later charged with an offence of s. 20 grievous bodily harm against WASHINGTON.

    Could DRISCOLL utilise the general defence of duress of circumstances in these circumstances?

    A No, DRISCOLL could not advance the defence as he was not in the situation where the threat to him was one of death or serious injury.
    B Yes, DRISCOLL would be able to use the defence as the offence that he is accused of committing is one that involves serious injury.
    C No, the defence is not available in answer to a charge of s. 20 grievous bodily harm.
    D Yes, the defence is available to DRISCOLL as he is charged with an offence involving causing injury to another—if it were a property-related charge then the defence would be unavailable.

36. Section 18(2) of the Modern Slavery Act 2015 allows a slavery and trafficking prevention order (STPO) to be made to prevent a person travelling to any specified country outside the United Kingdom, any country other than a country specified in the order or any country outside the United Kingdom.

    What is the maximum time that a prohibition order can be fixed initially and made by the court?

    A Four years.
    B Five years.
    C Six years.
    D Seven years.

37. AHLUWALIA believes that the aims of Babbar Khalsa (a proscribed international terrorist group) are justified and wants to further the activities of the group. Although AHLUWALIA is not a member of the Babbar Khalsa group, this does not stop him arranging a meeting in his house (a private residence) to which he invites five people. AHLUWALIA hopes to persuade those who attend the meeting to support Babbar Khalsa. Although five people were invited to the meeting, only two people turn up. This does not stop AHLUWALIA addressing the two men who attended about Babbar Khalsa.

    Does AHLUWALIA commit an offence under s. 12 of the Terrorism Act 2000 (supporting a proscribed organisation)?

    A No, the meeting was held in a private place not a public place.
    B Yes, merely by arranging a meeting of three or more people in public or private place to support a proscribed organisation, AHLUWALIA commits an offence under s. 12 of the Act.
    C No, the meeting that was arranged was not for five or more people.
    D Yes, but the offence is not committed until AHLUWALIA addresses the two men who were invited to his house.

38. CONRAD is sentenced to three years' imprisonment for an offence of burglary. He serves 18 months of the sentence and is then released. Several weeks after being released, CONRAD accompanies his friend, ZUCCARO, to a private estate where ZUCCARO is shooting (using a shotgun) in a competition. Whilst on the private estate, ZUCCARO asks CONRAD to hold on to his shotgun and a box of shotgun ammunition while he changes his clothes. CONRAD does so and several minutes later hands the shotgun and ammunition back to ZUCCARO.

    Does CONRAD commit an offence under s. 21 of the Firearms Act 1968 (possession of a firearm by a convicted person)?

    A Yes, CONRAD commits an offence in relation to the shotgun and the ammunition.
    B No, CONRAD does not commit an offence as s. 21 only applies to offenders who have been sentenced to imprisonment for five years or more.
    C Yes, CONRAD commits an offence but this would only be in respect of possession of the shotgun.
    D No, CONRAD does not commit an offence as the possession activity takes place on private land.

39. BANSKI is part of a coach tour visiting 'Needley Hall County House'. The house and grounds are all on private land. A large farm show is taking place on the land with lots of different commercial stands set up as part of the show. One of the stands is run by CHALMER who is a luxury car dealer who owns several expensive cars on display including an Audi Q7 motor vehicle. BANSKI examines the Q7 and although he does not have a driving licence, BANSKI asks CHALMER if he can drive it around the showground rather than arrange a test drive. CHALMER refuses the request. BANSKI sees the keys to the Q7 on a table near to the vehicle and takes them. He gets into the Q7 and starts the engine. He sits in the vehicle for 30 seconds with the engine running and then drives the vehicle out of the display area and slowly drives it around the area of the farm show. Even though he is being extremely careful, BANSKI causes a slight scratch to the driver's door of the Q7 as he drives it through a narrow gateway. He returns it to the display area where he is confronted by CHALMER. As he parks the Q7, he accidentally runs over CHALMER's foot causing severe bruising to CHALMER's foot.

    At what stage does BANSKI first commit the offence of aggravated vehicle taking (contrary to s. 12A of the Theft Act 1968)?

    A When he starts the engine of the vehicle.
    B When he drives the vehicle out of the display area.
    C When he causes damage to the vehicle.
    D When he causes injury to CHALMER.

40. WENTWORTH is a 17-year-old male who has been going out with SMYTH, a 15-year-old female, for three months and they have not had sex yet. One evening, whilst babysitting for SMYTH's older sister, they are alone. WENTWORTH, who knows that SMYTH does not want to risk having full sex as she is concerned about becoming pregnant, suggests that he uses a dildo on her. WENTWORTH knows SMYTH has a small dildo in her handbag. SMYTH is excited by the thought of WENTWORTH using the dildo on her and she agrees. WENTWORTH then uses the dildo on SMYTH.

    What would be the appropriate charge for WENTWORTH in these circumstances?

    A WENTWORTH commits an offence contrary to s. 3 of the Sexual Offences Act 2003.
    B WENTWORTH commits an offence contrary to s. 13 of the Sexual Offences Act 2003.
    C WENTWORTH commits an offence contrary to s. 9 of the Sexual Offences Act 2003.
    D Both WENTWORTH and SMYTH commit an offence contrary to s. 9 of the Sexual Offences Act 2003 as they are both under the age of 18.

41. LUMLEY, an adult male, is questioned by DC ATHERLEY with regard to two offences of burglary and he admits his part in the crimes. At court, he is sentenced to a hospital order owing to his drug habits and mental state. After four months he is released from hospital.

    There is no case to appeal, so in relation to the retention periods of relevant case material, how long does DC ATHERLEY need to retain the material?

    A Once LUMLEY is released, the case material can be disposed of as he served more than three months of a hospital order.
    B Once LUMLEY is released, the case material can be disposed of as there is no need to retain it when a hospital order has been given.
    C The material must be kept for at least 12 months after his release, if his sentence had been custodial; however, for hospital orders it only needs to be retained for six months from the date of release.
    D The material must be retained for a period of at least six months from the date of the hospital order.

42. PRASAD has been arrested in connection with an offence of attempted kidnapping. The victim states that when PRASAD tried to kidnap her he was not wearing a top of any description and she managed to scratch him on the chest with her fingernails. The victim states that the scratches were deep and left four large marks on the left side of PRASAD's chest. The officer in the case, DS JACKSON, wishes to examine PRASAD under s. 54A of the Police and Criminal Evidence Act 1984 (as amended by the Anti-terrorism, Crime and Security Act 2001), to ascertain whether or not he has such marks on his chest as their presence would tend to identify him as the person involved in the commission of the offence.

    Which of the following statements is correct?

    A The custody officer can authorise that PRASAD be examined without his consent but this must be authorised in writing.
    B PRASAD can be examined for the presence of the marks but only if he consents and an officer of the rank of inspector or above authorises the examination.
    C PRASAD cannot be examined as the Act allows only for the search and/or examination of an individual to establish their identification and not for evidence in relation to the offence for which they have been arrested.
    D An inspector must authorise the examination; authorisation can be given orally or in writing.

43. DC FAIRBAIRN is dealing with HAKIN who has been arrested for an offence of fraud. HAKIN has requested the services of his solicitor, TAYLOR, who arrives at the station and is taken into a consultation room where disclosure takes place. After TAYLOR has a consultation with HAKIN, an interview takes place. At the beginning of the interview DC FAIRBAIRN cautions HAKIN and asks if he understands the caution. At this point TAYLOR states that he has explained the meaning of the caution to his client and that his client fully understands the caution.

    What course of action should DC FAIRBAIRN take?

    A If it appears to DC FAIRBAIRN that HAKIN does not understand the caution, he should go on to explain it in his own words.
    B The fact that HAKIN has been told the meaning of the caution by his solicitor means that DC FAIRBAIRN need not go on to explain it.
    C As long as the caution has been given, then DC FAIRBAIRN may continue the interview without any further explanation of it.
    D Providing a record is made of the fact that the solicitor has explained the meaning of the caution to HAKIN, DC FAIRBAIRN need not go on to explain it.

44. BUTLER, a 23-year-old male, has attended the police station voluntarily to answer questions under caution. He is one of a number of staff being interviewed in respect of theft by employees at the DIY warehouse. At the end of the audio interview, although he has been cooperative in the interview, BUTLER refuses to sign the seal.

    Which of the statements below is the correct procedure in these circumstances?

    A The senior officer (by rank or length of service) in the interview room will sign the seal as BUTLER is not in police detention and has attended voluntarily.
    B An officer of at least the rank of inspector or if not available the custody officer or, if the suspect has not been arrested a sergeant shall be called into the interview room and asked to sign the seal.
    C An officer of at least the rank of inspector or if not available the custody officer must sign the seal.
    D An officer of at least the rank of inspector must sign the seal.

45. OGINSKY (aged 16 years) has been arrested for an offence of robbery (a recordable offence) and has been transported to the custody block of a designated police station. DC PIGDEN (the officer in the case) interviews OGINSKY in the presence of FARROW (who is OGINSKY's uncle and acting as an appropriate adult). During the interview, DC PIGDEN tells OGINSKY that he wishes to obtain footwear impressions from him (under s. 61A of the Police and Criminal Evidence Act 1984) and asks for his consent—OGINSKY refuses.

    Can DC PIGDEN obtain footwear samples from OGINSKY in these circumstances?

    A No, as footwear samples can only be obtained from a person in police detention with their written consent.
    B Yes, and DC PIGDEN can use force to obtain them if necessary.
    C No, unless FARROW provides written consent for DC PIGDEN to obtain footwear impressions from OGINSKY.
    D Yes, if the impressions are necessary to prove or disprove OGINSKY's involvement in the robbery offence.

46. ROBERTS, an adult female, is walking along a lane and sees a gated doorway which is the entrance to the rear garden of a large house. She is a bit hungry after her walk and thinks there may be some fruit she could eat within the garden walls. She enters the garden (as a trespasser) and she can see there is an array of raspberry bushes in fruit further up the garden. As ROBERTS walks up the garden, she sees a young man CORBETT sunbathing in his shorts; ROBERTS changes her mind about the fruit and approaches him with the intention of sexually touching him in the genital area of his shorts for a joke. When she gets closer, a large dog barks and awakes CORBETT and ROBERTS runs out of the garden.

    Does ROBERTS commit the offence of trespass with intent to commit a relevant sexual offence (contrary to s. 63 of the Sexual Offences Act 2003)?

    A Yes, but only if she actually carried out her intentions to touch CORBETT whilst she is a trespasser.
    B No, ROBERTS does not commit the offence as the garden is not premises for the purposes of s. 63.
    C Yes, ROBERTS commits the offence as the intent to commit a relevant sexual offence can come about after entry as a trespasser and a garden is premises for the purposes of s. 63.
    D No, ROBERTS does not commit the offence because the intent for the relevant sexual offence needs to be formed before entry to the premises as a trespasser.

47. PC WHITLEY is making enquiries regarding an offence of robbery that has just taken place at a bookmakers. The officer is visiting shops that are in the same street as the bookmakers and is looking for witnesses to the offence. He enters a florists shop which is situated opposite the bookmakers and speaks to STREDWICK who is working behind the serving counter. When PC WHITLEY asks STREDWICK if she has seen anything, she replies, *'I don't have to tell you anything, you pig!'* PC WHITLEY asks STREDWICK to be reasonable and help if she can, to which STREDWICK responds, *'OK, the bloke responsible was wearing a green jacket and ran off towards the town hall'*. This is deliberately misleading information provided by STREDWICK as the offender was wearing a different colour jacket and ran off in the opposite direction to that which she said he did.

Does STREDWICK commit the offence of obstructing a police officer (contrary to s. 89(2) of the Police Act 1996)?

A No, as STREDWICK does not offer any form of physical resistance to PC WHITLEY.
B Yes, when she tells PC WHITLEY she does not have to tell him anything and also when she provides the deliberately misleading information.
C No, as this offence can only be committed by a person who is under a positive obligation to assist the police and STREDWICK is not in that position.
D Yes, but only when she provides the deliberately misleading information to PC WHITLEY.

48. CRANSHAW and GUBBIN work for a large insurance company. CRANSHAW supervises GUBBIN but the two do not get on at all resulting in several heated disagreements. GUBBIN wants to punish CRANSHAW and knows that CRANSHAW has her lunch in a nearby pub each day. He has a chat with POLLOCK (his friend) and encourages POLLOCK to assault CRANSHAW in the pub as a favour to him. POLLOCK agrees and GUBBIN provides a description of CRANSHAW to POLLOCK. POLLOCK goes into the pub, sees CRANSHAW and punches her in the face causing her injury. POLLOCK aims another punch at CRANSHAW who ducks out of the way causing POLLOCK to strike and injure BUTTON who is an innocent bystander. On his way out of the pub, POLLOCK sees EDGE who he has had personal disagreements with and he attacks EDGE causing EDGE serious injury.

Considering the liability of GUBBIN and the doctrine of transferred *mens rea*, which of the following comments is correct?

A GUBBIN would be liable for the assault injuries to CRANSHAW alone.
B GUBBIN would be liable for the assault injuries to CRANSHAW and BUTTON but not for the assault injuries sustained by EDGE.
C GUBBIN would be liable for the assault injuries to CRANSHAW and EDGE but not for the assault injuries sustained by BUTTON.
D GUBBIN would be liable for the assault injuries sustained by CRANSHAW, BUTTON and EDGE.

49. BARON is staying at his friend's address whilst his friend is on holiday. BARON has full use of the house and is allowed to bring his friend, STRETTON, to the house if he wishes. BARON and STRETTON are in the lounge of the house watching a football match between their team and their fierce local rivals in the FA Cup. During the match a defender from the team BARON and STRETTON support makes a mistake allowing the opposition to score a goal. The defender who made the error is a black male and BARON shouts out *'You stupid black bastard; fuck off home to your mud hut'*. This is shouted so loud that a number of people standing at a bus stop outside the house hear what is said and are extremely offended. BARON's intention is to stir up racial hatred in STRETTON and he had no idea that his comments could be heard outside the house.

    In relation to using of words or behaviour or display of written materials (contrary to s. 18 of the Public Order Act 1986) does BARON commit an offence?

    A Yes, he commits the offence and in these circumstances would not have a defence.
    B No, as s. 18 only applies to activities carried out in a public place not a private dwelling.
    C No, because he intended to stir up racial hatred in STRETTON who was also in the same dwelling.
    D Yes, he commits the offence but would have a defence available if he can prove he was inside a dwelling and had no reason to believe that his words would be heard by a person outside that or any other dwelling.

50. CHUKKA decides to carry out a robbery at a post office. He believes he will have to threaten or possibly even use force in order to carry out the offence so he purchases a sawn-off shotgun to threaten staff with. He travels to the post office and parks his car a short distance away. He places the sawn-off shotgun into a bag and walks towards the post office. He enters the post office and approaches the counter and threatens a member of staff with the sawn-off shotgun. The member of staff presses an alarm button and CHUKKA flees the scene empty-handed.

    At what point would CHUKKA attract liability for an attempt to commit robbery (under s. 1 of the Criminal Attempts Act 1981)?

    A When he purchases the shotgun to threaten the staff with.
    B When he travels to the post office and parks a short distance away.
    C When he places the sawn-off shotgun into a bag and walks towards the post office.
    D When he approaches the counter and threatens the member of staff with the sawn-off shotgun.

51. BEATON owns and works in a small jewellery shop. LANE walks into the shop and approaches BEATON and holds up a mobile phone which shows live images of BEATON's wife at their home address five miles from the jewellery shop, with a gun to her head (the gun is being held by TAYLOR who is LANE's accomplice). LANE tells BEATON to hand over all the jewellery in the shop and any cash he has or his wife will be shot. BEATON refuses. LANE tells TAYLOR to hurt BEATON's wife and TAYLOR punches her in the face. LANE repeats his demand and BEATON hands over all the jewellery and cash he has.

    Has an offence of robbery (contrary to s. 8 of the Theft Act 1968) been committed in these circumstances?

    A No, as the force used was not used at the scene of the theft.
    B Yes, the offence is committed when BEATON is shown the image of his wife with the gun to her head.
    C No, as the threatened force or the force used was not towards or on BEATON (the shop owner).
    D Yes, the offence is committed when BEATON's wife is subject to force and the jewellery and cash is stolen.

52. PC ARROW is directed to attend a call where it is reported that a person is behaving suspiciously around some farm buildings. The officer arrives at the scene and sees PURLEY walking out of a farm building and across a field. There is a very large sign next to the field indicating that it is private property. As PURLEY climbs over a fence and into the road, PC ARROW stops him. PURLEY admits he was looking for somewhere to sleep for the night and was trespassing. The officer searches PURLEY and finds an air pistol in his possession. PC ARROW arrests PURLEY in respect of his commission of an offence of trespassing with a firearm on land (contrary to s. 20(2) of the Firearms Act 1968 and using the provisions of s. 24 of the Police and Criminal Evidence Act 1984). PC ARROW now wishes to use the provisions of s. 32 of the Police and Criminal Evidence Act 1984 to search PURLEY and the nearby farm building.

    With regard to the officer's powers under s. 32 of the Police and Criminal Evidence Act 1984, which of the following comments is true?

    A PC ARROW cannot search the farm building that PURLEY was seen walking out from under s. 32 of the Act.
    B PC ARROW has a power under s. 32 to search PURLEY for evidence but only for evidence specifically relating to the offence for which he was arrested.
    C PC ARROW may require PURLEY to remove his outer coat, jacket and gloves for the purpose of the search but he could not search in PURLEY's mouth.
    D If PC ARROW suspects that PURLEY may present a danger to himself or others then he may search him.

53. CORCORAN (who is 20 years old) is sitting outside a school in his car and decides to smoke some cannabis (a Class B drug). As it is 11:00 hours and classes are taking place at the school, a number of school pupils and several members of staff at the school see what is going on. Staff alert the police and PC WHITE is sent to the incident. Before the officer arrives, SHAW (who is 17 years old and a friend of CORCORAN's), walks past CORCORAN and the two start a conversation. After several minutes, CORCORAN finishes smoking the cannabis and just then PC WHITE arrives in a marked police vehicle. As the officer arrives, CORCORAN panics and hands SHAW a large bag of cannabis saying, 'I want to smoke this later so look after it for me and I'll pay you £20.' SHAW knows that he is being handed cannabis and agrees and walks away and watches as PC WHITE searches CORCORAN and his car. Finding nothing, the officer leaves. SHAW walks back to CORCORAN and returns the cannabis to him. CORCORAN gives £20 to SHAW and drives off.

    Considering the offence of supplying a controlled drug (contrary to s. 4(3) of the Misuse of Drugs Act 1971) and the law in relation to that offence, which of the following comments is correct?

    A CORCORAN and SHAW are guilty of the offence. Because of the time and place of the offence, the court will be required to consider 'aggravating' factors (under s. 4A of the Act) in relation to CORCORAN only.

    B CORCORAN and SHAW are guilty of the offence. Because of the time and place of the offence, the court will be required to consider 'aggravating' factors (under s. 4A of the Act) in relation to both men.

    C Only CORCORAN is guilty of the offence. Because of the time and place of the offence, the court will be required to consider 'aggravating' factors (under s. 4A of the Act) in relation to it.

    D Only SHAW is guilty of the offence. As he is under 18 years of age the court will not consider the offence 'aggravated' (under s. 4A of the Act).

54. PURCELL is suspected of carrying out a minor assault on BROWN. PC GREALEY is investigating the case and asks PURCELL to attend a police station to be interviewed regarding the assault. PC GREALEY does not arrest PURCELL who, although told of all his rights, states that he does not need or want any legal advice. During the interview, PC GREALEY notices a medium-sized tear in the fabric of a coat that PURCELL is wearing and believes that this may be attributable to PURCELL's participation in the assault. PC GREALEY asks PURCELL to account for the tear and PURCELL states that he did it when he was leaving his house that morning by catching it on a door frame. PC GREALEY does not believe PURCELL.

    Could PC GREALEY give PURCELL a 'special warning' (under s. 36 of the Criminal Justice and Public Order Act 1994) in relation to the damage to his coat?

    A Yes, as PC GREALEY does not believe the account that PURCELL gives in relation to the damage to his coat.

    B No, as PURCELL has not been arrested.

    C Yes, although the 'special warning' must be given to PURCELL immediately after his response to the question(s) regarding the damage to his coat.

    D No, as PURCELL does not have a solicitor with him in the interview.

55. BROWN has been charged with an offence of burglary and has been bailed by PS KING (the custody officer). PS KING imposed a number of bail conditions upon BROWN, including a curfew between set times. One week after being bailed, BROWN finds out that his girlfriend is pregnant and wants to have his bail condition of curfew modified so that he can help his girlfriend during her pregnancy.

    Which of the following comments is correct in respect of varying the bail condition?

    A BROWN must speak to PS KING who is the only person who can vary the conditions of bail.
    B BROWN's conditions of bail can be varied by PS KING or another custody officer serving at any police station in PS KING's force area.
    C BROWN's conditions of bail can be varied by PS KING or another custody officer serving at the same police station that PS KING works at.
    D BROWN's conditions of bail can be varied but only by a magistrates' court.

56. MILBURN (a 47-year-old male) establishes contact with FOSTER (a 15-year-old female) using an internet video communication service. MILBURN lies about his age to FOSTER telling her that he is 15 years old but manages to get away with this by telling FOSTER his webcam has a fault and covering it so that he cannot be seen (although he can be heard). During the conversation, MILBURN asks FOSTER if she is 'still a virgin' and then begins to masturbate, telling FOSTER what he is doing in the process. MILBURN does this to obtain sexual gratification.

    Which of the following comments is correct in relation to the offence of engaging in sexual activity in the presence of a child (contrary to s. 11 of the Sexual Offences Act 2003)?

    A The offence would not be committed by MILBURN as FOSTER cannot see him masturbating.
    B The activity must take place in the physical presence of the child; this has not occurred so the offence is incomplete.
    C MILBURN commits the offence in these circumstances.
    D The offence is not committed as FOSTER is 15 years old (it must be in the hearing and/or presence of a child under 13).

57. MALPASS and FROBISHER are friends and have a bet between each other. MALPASS bets £500 that FROBISHER would not have the nerve to pick up a prostitute and have sex with her. FROBISHER takes the bet and the two men drive to an area that is well known to be frequented by prostitutes. FROBISHER drops MALPASS off on a street corner so that he can witness what happens. FROBISHER then drives to the other side of the road and winds his car window down to speak to WARNER who is standing on the street corner dressed provocatively. FROBISHER asks WARNER to get into his car to 'discuss terms' and WARNER complies. Once inside the car, WARNER tells FROBISHER that sexual intercourse is £100. FROBISHER tells her that is too much and at this point locks the doors of the car and tells WARNER to drop her price or he will not let her go. WARNER panics and tells FROBISHER to let her out. FROBISHER repeats his demand that she drop her price so WARNER says she will drop it to £50; FROBISHER tells her it is still too much. At this point, WARNER starts to scream so FROBISHER unlocks the doors and tells WARNER to get out. She does so and FROBISHER drives away.

    Does FROBISHER commit the offence of false imprisonment (contrary to common law)?

    A Yes, FROBISHER commits the offence when he locks the doors of his car and restrains WARNER's freedom of movement.
    B No, FROBISHER does not commit the offence as he has not touched WARNER and has therefore not physically restrained her freedom of movement.
    C Yes, FROBISHER commits the offence but the prosecution would have to prove that he intended to restrain WARNER's freedom of movement, as recklessness in respect of this element of the offence is not enough.
    D No, FROBISHER does not commit the offence as WARNER's freedom of movement was only restrained for a very short period of time.

58. CATO (aged 17) is involved in a car accident and is rushed to the accident and emergency ward of a nearby hospital for treatment. CATO has suffered significant harm as a consequence of being involved in the accident and is receiving treatment for his injuries when his parents arrive. CATO's parents are adamant that they do not want CATO to stay at the hospital as a relative of theirs has recently died in hospital having been admitted for a minor operation and then contracting the MRSA 'superbug'. CATO's parents are causing a disturbance at the hospital, demanding that they be allowed to take their son away and treat him at their home. The police are called to the incident and PC BUCKINGHAM attends the incident.

    With regard to police powers under s. 46 of the Children Act 1989, which of the following comments is true?

    A The powers under s. 46 cannot be used by the officer as CATO is 17 years old.
    B If PC BUCKINGHAM has reasonable cause to believe that CATO would otherwise be likely to suffer serious harm, he may take such steps as are reasonable to prevent CATO being removed from the hospital.
    C PC BUCKINGHAM can take such steps as are reasonable to prevent CATO's removal from the hospital if he has the authority of an officer of at least the rank of inspector to do so.
    D If PC BUCKINGHAM reasonably believes that the continued presence of CATO's parents may result in serious harm to CATO, he can remove the parents from the hospital premises.

59. FELL (who is 18 years old) and SAYER (who is 17 years old) have been arrested in connection with an offence of robbery. The officer in charge of the case, DC HEINZMAN, has information and evidence that FELL and SAYER are responsible for a large number of other robbery offences and wishes to speak to them about these offences. As such, DC HEINZMAN seeks to have FELL and SAYER remanded into police custody under s. 128 of the Magistrates' Courts Act 1980 so that he can speak to them about the other robbery offences.

    Which of the following comments is correct in relation to such a remand?

    A FELL could be remanded in police custody for a period not exceeding three clear days; SAYER could be remanded in police custody for a period not exceeding 24 hours.
    B FELL could be remanded in police custody for a period not exceeding three clear days; SAYER could not be remanded in police custody as he is a juvenile.
    C FELL and SAYER could be remanded in police custody for a period not exceeding three clear days.
    D FELL and SAYER could be remanded in police custody for a period not exceeding 24 hours.

60. FIELD is a 12-year-old girl and is attracted to her piano teacher McNULTY who provides private tuition to FIELD at his home address. For some time FIELD's mother accompanied her to her lessons; however, as FIELD has been having lessons for three years with McNULTY her mother now allows her to go on her own. FIELD is physically well developed for her age, however McNULTY is aware of her true age. During a piano lesson FIELD asks McNULTY to touch her legs up to her pants. McNULTY flatly refuses and tells her not to be so silly. FIELD says to McNULTY, 'Well, I really want you to have sex with me, to be my first.' At this, she stands up and removes her pants; McNULTY, shocked and worried, leaves the room immediately.

    Considering s. 44 of the Serious Crime Act 2007 (intentionally encouraging or assisting an offence), is FIELD liable?

    A FIELD is not guilty in these circumstances as rape would be committed if McNULTY had sex with her, which is for her own protection.
    B FIELD does commit the offence as she is over the age of 10 years, the age of criminal responsibility.
    C FIELD is not guilty in these circumstances as the act she encouraged did not take place.
    D FIELD is guilty of the offence but in the circumstances it would be an attempt owing to her age being under 13.

61. The Sexual Offences (Amendment) Act 1992 allows the victim anonymity in sexual offence cases.

    In relation to this legislation, which of the following statements is correct regarding offences of sexual assault by touching?

    A The victim is entitled to anonymity until the end of the trial or any appeal.
    B The victim is entitled to anonymity indefinitely.
    C The victim is entitled to anonymity throughout their lifetime.
    D Anonymity does not apply to the offence of sexual assault by touching.

62. David HOWE and Jane HOWE are husband and wife and have separated after David found out that Jane was having an affair. Whilst they arrange the sale of the matrimonial home to split the proceeds, Jane is living in the matrimonial home and David is renting a flat. The situation between the two has deteriorated and they are arguing over who owns what in the matrimonial home. One evening, whilst Jane is out, David visits the matrimonial home with his friend FISHER. They force the front door of the house and remove several items of property, including a fridge and a television, from the house. David HOWE is convinced that he has every right to the property as he paid for it and FISHER believes that he is helping David exercise a lawful right. Whilst FISHER is outside the house loading the van they drove to the house in, David HOWE sees a watch that he knows belongs to Jane and decides to take it for revenge and leaves the house.

    Which of the following statements is correct in respect of the law relating to the Theft Act 1968?

    A David HOWE could be charged with theft (s. 1) in relation to the watch but such a prosecution may only be instituted against him with the consent of the Director of Public Prosecutions.
    B FISHER has committed an offence of burglary (s. 9(1)(a)) when he enters the house with David HOWE.
    C David HOWE could be charged with burglary (s. 9(1)(b)) of the watch.
    D No offence under the Theft Act has been committed by either man in this situation.

63. MILES is walking in the red light area of the city because he is considering paying for the services of a prostitute. On one of the street corners he sees CALDERSHAW, a prostitute, plying her trade. MILES realises that he has come out of the house with no cash so he decides to rape CALDERSHAW instead. MILES punches CALDERSHAW in the face and she falls to the ground and he can see clearly that she has no pants on. However, out of the top pocket of her denim jacket a large amount of cash falls to the ground near to her. MILES changes his mind, picks up the cash and runs off. A short time later he sees NOWAKOWSKI looking into a shop window and he can see her purse sticking out of her handbag so he decides to steal it. MILES places his hand on the purse and picks it out of her handbag, of which NOWAKOWSKI is totally unaware. At that moment a person behind MILES accidentally bumps into him and in turn he accidentally pushes NOWAKOWSKI into the shop window causing a deep wound to her face. MILES makes good his escape.

    Considering only the offence of robbery (contrary to s. 8 of the Theft Act 1968), which of the following statements is correct?

    A MILES commits robbery only with regards to CALDERSHAW.
    B MILES commits robbery only with regard to NOWAKOWSKI.
    C MILES commits robbery against both CALDERSHAW and NOWAKOWSKI.
    D MILES does not commit any robbery offence.

64. Magistrates have made a 'live link bail' direction (under s. 57C of the Crime and Disorder Act 1998) in relation to CRABTREE (a male defendant) who is being prosecuted for a number of different offences. CRABTREE has been directed to attend the preliminary hearing of his case through a live link at a police station and duly attends the police station at the appointed time. PCs SAMUEL (a male police officer) and ORWELL (a female designated detention officer) are directed to deal with CRABTREE and want to know the extent of their powers to search CRABTREE under s. 54B of the Police and Criminal Evidence Act 1984.

    Which of the following statements is true with regard to the power under s. 54B?

    A Either officer may search CRABTREE although seizure of items found as a consequence of the search can only take place if the searching officer reasonably believes the thing to be seized is evidence of an offence.

    B The power of search under s. 54B is available to PC SAMUEL only as he is a male police officer; it is not available to designated detention officers.

    C Any police officer or designated detention officer may use the search power. The sex of the police officer or designated detention officer is irrelevant.

    D Only PC SAMUEL may search CRABTREE; the officer may also search any article CRABTREE has in his possession. If CRABTREE refuses to be searched, he can be arrested.

65. MICHAM has been arrested in relation to an offence of robbery. He denies any involvement in the offence, disputing the identification evidence. MICHAM has indicated that he will not take part in any video identification or identification parade so consideration is being given to a group identification process.

    Considering Annex C of Code D of the Codes of Practice (dealing with group identification), which of the following statements is correct?

    A A group identification may only take place with MITCHAM's consent and cooperation.
    B A group identification process can take place at a police station.
    C A group identification process must involve a moving (not stationary) group.
    D A group identification process must be video recorded in all circumstances.

66. PC BRIDIE has arrested CHUNTAO for an offence of burglary and has taken him to a designated police station. PC BRIDIE wants to search a flat which is owned by CHUNTAO for evidence in connection with the burglary CHUNTAO has been arrested for.

    Which of the following comments is correct in relation to the use of the power under s. 18 of the Police and Criminal Evidence Act 1984 in this situation?

    A PC BRIDIE must have reasonable grounds to suspect that there is evidence on the premises relating to the burglary or some other indictable offence which is connected to the burglary or similar to it. If that is the case, an officer of the rank of inspector or above could provide an oral authorisation for the use of the s. 18 power.

    B PC BRIDIE must have reasonable grounds to believe that there is evidence on the premises relating to the burglary or some other indictable offence which is connected to the burglary or similar to it. If that is the case, an officer of the rank of inspector or above could provide a written authorisation for the use of the s. 18 power.

    C PC BRIDIE must have reasonable grounds to believe that there is evidence on the premises relating to the burglary or some other indictable offence which is connected to the burglary or similar to it. If that is the case, an officer of the rank of inspector or above could provide an oral authorisation for the use of the s. 18 power.

    D PC BRIDIE must have reasonable grounds to suspect that there is evidence on the premises relating to the burglary or some other indictable offence which is connected to the burglary or similar to it. If that is the case, an officer of the rank of inspector or above could provide a written authorisation for the use of the s. 18 power.

67. CALLAGHAN drives onto the forecourt of a motorway service station and whilst filling his car with fuel sees RICE, a hitchhiker, holding a sign stating 'Lift to London?' CALLAGHAN is attracted to RICE and approaches her and states he will give her a lift. RICE accepts and gets in to the front passenger seat of CALLAGHAN's car. CALLAGHAN drives off the forecourt onto the motorway. The two engage in conversation as CALLAGHAN drives along the slip road towards the motorway and just before the vehicle joins the motorway CALLAGHAN tells RICE *'Now I've got you, I'm going to fuck you whether you like it or not!'* and grabs hold of RICE's right breast. RICE is petrified and thinks she is going to be raped. She opens the passenger door and jumps out of the vehicle, breaking her arm as she hits the surface of the road.

    Considering the legal concepts regarding an intervening act, which of the comments below is correct?

    A CALLAGHAN cannot be held responsible for the actions of RICE which result in her injury as he did not directly inflict them.

    B CALLAGHAN can be held liable for the injury caused to RICE if a court considers her actions might reasonably have been anticipated in such a situation.

    C CALLAGHAN could only be held liable for the injuries to RICE if he considered they might take place as a result of his actions.

    D CALLAGHAN cannot be held responsible for the injuries caused to RICE as RICE brought them about of her own volition (opening the car door and jumping out of the vehicle).

68. BANKS is an adult male and he falsely imprisons both WEST, an adult male, and CARTER, an adult female. BANKS has lured them to his house on the pretext that he is thinking of selling the property knowing that they are both interested in buying his house with their respective partners. BANKS locks all the doors to the property and produces a large sword. Both WEST and CARTER are very scared and when he requests that they both remove their clothes they do so. BANKS then tells WEST to put his penis into CARTER's mouth and insert his fingers in her vagina. Initially WEST refuses but after threats with the sword both WEST and CARTER submit to BANKS's requests.

    Considering only offences contrary to the Sexual Offences Act 2003, which of the statements below is correct with regards to the criminal responsibility of all parties?

    A BANKS commits an offence of causing sexual activity without consent and WEST commits two offences of rape.
    B BANKS would be guilty of causing sexual activity without consent if it could be shown that it was for sexual gratification.
    C BANKS commits the offence of causing sexual activity without consent.
    D BANKS commits causing sexual activity without consent and WEST commits rape and assault by penetration.

69. RUTTER is having problems with her boss PATTERSON who has put her on an action plan to improve RUTTER's professional skills. RUTTER believes this is unjustified, which it is not, and therefore decides to cause PATTERSON anxiety or distress. RUTTER sends PATTERSON a false letter from a solicitor stating that PATTERSON is being taken to court by a nearby neighbour for the noise her dog makes in the garden in the morning. RUTTER also sends a text from an unidentified mobile phone stating that PATTERSON's daughter has been involved in a minor accident at school. RUTTER also puts dog faeces through PATTERSON's letterbox.

    Considering the offences under s. 1(1) of the Malicious Communications Act 1988, which, if any, offences have been committed?

    A None of the acts by RUTTER are covered by this legislation.
    B RUTTER only commits the offence when she sends the false letter.
    C RUTTER only commits the offence when she sends the false letter and the text.
    D RUTTER commits the offence on all three occasions.

70. POTOLI and VERRITT are civil partners who have been having problems with ROSS (who frequents a pub that POTOLI and VERRITT visit). ROSS constantly directs abuse at POTOLI and VERRITT about their sexuality and the pair have had enough. They decide that ROSS needs to be taught a lesson and agree that they will attack him (although they do not intend to cause him any more than very minor harm, i.e. a common battery). The two plan the offence so that there will be no witnesses and so that ROSS will not be able to identify them as the offenders. On the night of the planned offence, they leave their house and wait for ROSS in an alleyway at the side of the pub. Whilst waiting, POTOLI has second thoughts about committing the offence and tells VERRITT that he does not want to go through with their plan. VERRITT states that he understands and that they should forget their plan. The two men return to their home and ROSS is not subject to any harm by the pair. As it turns out, ROSS could not possibly have been assaulted as he was not drinking in the pub that evening—he was on holiday in Poland.

    Considering only the offence of statutory conspiracy (contrary to s. 1 of the Criminal Law Act 1977), which of the following comments is correct?

    A A conspiracy offence does not exist as you can only conspire to commit an indictable offence and an offence of 'common battery' under s. 39 of the Criminal Justice Act 1988 is an offence that is triable summarily.
    B A conspiracy offence has not been committed as there was never any 'end product' as a consequence of the agreement between the two men.
    C A conspiracy offence has not been committed as it was impossible for ROSS to be assaulted as he was in Poland at the time the two men planned to assault him.
    D No conspiracy offence has been committed as the two participants are civil partners.

71. PUGH is owed £200 by CANNON. PUGH has spoken to CANNON about the debt on several occasions but there is no sign of CANNON paying the money back. PUGH has become frustrated by this situation and decides that enough is enough and the next time he sees CANNON he will get his money. He sees CANNON walking along a street and confronts him demanding that the debt be repaid. CANNON becomes annoyed and tells PUGH he will never repay the money. PUGH produces a knife and holds it to CANNON's face and tells him that unless he pays the debt he will be stabbed. PUGH knows the means he is using to get the debt repaid is wrong but believes he has a lawful right to have the debt repaid. CANNON refuses, so PUGH cuts CANNON across the face to encourage him to pay up. CANNON panics and hands over £200 from his wallet to PUGH as settlement for the debt. Satisfied that the debt has been settled, PUGH walks away.

    At what point, if at all, has the offence of robbery been committed?

    A The offence of robbery has not been committed in these circumstances.
    B When PUGH produces the knife and holds it to CANNON's face.
    C When PUGH uses the knife to cut CANNON across his face.
    D When CANNON hands the £200 to PUGH.

72. POPESCU, an adult male, has been arrested for several offences of burglary and you intend to search properties that may have evidence relating to the offences that POPESCU has been arrested for. POPESCU occupies a house at 22 Cross Avenue, which he rents from the estate agents Manning and Sons and he also owns and controls a lock-up garage which he uses to keep his car in. You have intelligence at your disposal which indicates POPESCU rents a storage facility in a warehouse but this is unconfirmed and you only reasonably suspect he controls the storage facility.

With the correct authorisation from an inspector or above, which of the following statements is correct as to which properties can be searched by a constable under s. 18 of PACE 1984?

A All three properties can be searched.
B The storage facility and the house he rents.
C The house he rents and his garage.
D Only the house he rents.

73. MIFFLIN is a hypochondriac and believes that she has a serious condition which is causing her a great deal of pain (this is not true). She visits her local surgery and speaks with her general practitioner, Dr PATTEN, and asks for a pain-killing injection to ease her suffering. Dr PATTEN refuses the injection as he is aware of MIFFLIN's hypochondria and knows that she is not in any pain. MIFFLIN tells Dr PATTEN that if he does not provide her with the pain-killing injection, she will leave the surgery and slash all the tyres on his expensive sports car which is parked directly outside the surgery. Dr PATTEN believes MIFFLIN and provides her with the pain-killing injection.

Which of the following is true?

A This is not a case of blackmail as there has been no 'gain' or 'loss' in property.
B The offence of blackmail is committed at the moment MIFFLIN makes the demand for the pain-killing injection accompanied by the threats to damage Dr PATTEN's car.
C This is not a case of blackmail as the menaces were not threatened 'then and there'; the damage was going to take place at another time and in another place.
D The offence of blackmail is committed at the moment Dr PATTEN provides the pain-killing injection to MIFFLIN.

74. PC VERRIN arrests WATERFIELD for failing to take part in a preliminary screening test (for the purposes of drink/drive offences under the Road Traffic Act 1988). Unfortunately, the arrest was unlawful as PC VERRIN was a trespasser on land owned by WATERFIELD when the arrest was made. After the arrest, PC VERRIN takes hold of WATERFIELD and a struggle ensues during which PC VERRIN is assaulted by WATERFIELD resulting in PC VERRIN sustaining several small cuts and bruises to his left arm. Other officers arrive at the scene and WATERFIELD is escorted to a designated police station where he is brought in to the custody block and placed in front of the custody officer, PS BLACKBURN. When PS BLACKBURN asks WATERFIELD for his name, WATERFIELD responds by telling the officer to *'Fuck off'* and punching PS BLACKBURN in the face, causing minor bruising to PS BLACKBURN's face.

    Has an offence of assault police (contrary to s. 89(1) of the Police Act 1996) been committed?

    A No, the arrest made by PC VERRIN was unlawful. This means that any action by the police following an unlawful arrest (including that of the custody officer) cannot be regarded as that of an officer carrying out the lawful execution of his/her duty.
    B Yes, the offence has been committed upon PC VERRIN and PS BLACKBURN.
    C No, as the injuries received by both officers are minor.
    D Yes, but only upon PS BLACKBURN.

75. NELSON is an 18-year-old male and his new girlfriend is LENNON, a 15-year-old female (NELSON is aware of LENNON's age). They have been going out together for a couple of weeks. LENNON is very shy and knows very little about sex. NELSON decides that the only way he is going to be able to have sex with LENNON is to show her pictures of a pornographic nature to lower her inhibitions so he can achieve sexual gratification at a later date. NELSON at first shows LENNON cartoon still images of persons having sexual intercourse. Then a day later he shows her moving cartoons of persons having sexual intercourse. A week later as LENNON is now showing more interest, NELSON shows her a pornographic video involving sexual intercourse between males and females via the internet. NELSON believes that after this showing she will have sex with him. LENNON is not amused by this and tells him their relationship is over.

    Considering the offence under s. 12 of the Sexual Offences Act 2003 (causing a child to watch a sex act) when if at all does NELSON first commit the offence?

    A NELSON does not commit the offence as no sexual gratification was obtained whilst LENNON was exposed to the pornography.
    B NELSON commits the offence when he showed her the internet pornography as that was when he believed he would obtain sexual gratification.
    C NELSON commits the offence when he shows the moving cartoon pornography.
    D NELSON commits the offence when he shows LENNON the first pornographic cartoon still image.

76. CAFFERATTA is convicted of an offence under s. 4(2) of the Misuse of Drugs Act 1971 (production of a controlled drug) and is sentenced to a period of three years in prison.

    In these circumstances, can a court impose a travel restriction order on CAFFERATTA (under s. 33 of the Criminal Justice and Police Act 2001)?

    A Yes, and if imposed the order must run for a minimum of three years.
    B Yes, although the maximum period the order can run for is five years.
    C No, as CAFFERATTA has not been sentenced to a period of imprisonment of four or more years.
    D No, as production of a controlled drug under s. 4(2) of the Misuse of Drugs Act 1971 is not classed as a 'drug trafficking offence'.

77. BARKER is a tramp who travels from place to place, sleeping in the streets. On a particularly cold night, BARKER becomes concerned that he may die from hypothermia so purely to obtain shelter from the cold he breaks into a warehouse office. Once inside the office, he turns on an electric fire to warm himself up. Having warmed up, he decides to look around the office to see if there is anything worth stealing and after a short search he finds a jar containing approximately £30 in change which he steals. Curious about the premises he is in, he moves from the warehouse office through a door into a room marked 'Stores'. He walks around the store for several minutes before becoming bored and frustrated at his lot in life and he damages a sink unit in the store. As he is about to leave, he sees a small box containing a number of batteries and, thinking he will be able to sell them, he steals them.

    At what stage does BARKER first commit an offence of burglary under s. 9(1)(a) or s. 9(1)(b) of the Theft Act 1968?

    A A burglary offence is first committed when BARKER turns on the electric fire.
    B A burglary offence is first committed when BARKER steals the £30 in change.
    C A burglary offence is first committed when BARKER damages the sink.
    D A burglary offence is first committed when BARKER steals the batteries.

78. OLDHAM has fallen out with his next-door neighbour, JANKOWSKI (who is Polish), regarding the noise made by a party held at JANKOWSKI's house. A couple of days after the party, OLDHAM sees JANKOWSKI leave his house with his dog and, aware that JANKOWSKI will be out walking his dog for some time, OLDHAM approaches JANKOWSKI's car. In order to demonstrate his hostility towards JANKOWSKI and for revenge for the noise of the party, OLDHAM uses a can of spray paint to spray 'Fuck Off Polish Twat!' on one side of the car and 'Bloody Foreigners Leave Now!' on the other side of the car. OLDHAM is later arrested in relation to the criminal damage.

    Considering s. 28 of the Crime and Disorder Act 1998, would this be considered to be a racially aggravated offence?

    A No, as JANKOWSKI was not present when the criminal damage took place.
    B Yes, the words sprayed on both sides of the car would be considered racially aggravated.
    C No, as criminal damage (under s. 1(1) of the Criminal Damage Act 1971) is not an offence that is covered by s. 28 of the Crime and Disorder Act 1998.
    D Yes, but only in relation to the words 'Fuck Off Polish Twat'.

79. DC HOLTOM is putting a file together in relation to a case of rape where the offender has pleaded 'not guilty' and the case is going to be heard in Crown Court. The officer is being assisted by TI SINGH. TI SINGH asks a number of questions about the evidence in the case particularly relating to its weight and admissibility in court. The officers disagree on several elements of this area of law and their supervisor, DS RABY steps in to correct their misunderstanding.

    Considering the issues in relation to the weight and admissibility of evidence, which of the following comments is correct?

    A TI SINGH states evidence can be excluded if its prejudicial effect outweighs its probative value.
    B DC HOLTOM states that the question of admissibility of evidence is a question of fact to be decided by members of a jury.
    C TI SINGH states that evidence cannot be excluded based on the incompetence of a witness.
    D DC HOLTOM states that evidence can only be excluded via the use of s. 76 of the Police and Criminal Evidence Act 1984.

80. MOSS wants to have sexual intercourse with a prostitute. He is aware that East House Road (which is about three miles from his home) has a strong reputation for prostitution activities and he gets into his car and drives to the location. MOSS drives up and down East House Road for 10 minutes and can see that there are a number of women standing outside the front door of a house on the road. MOSS makes the assumption that they are all prostitutes and pulls up next to the women in his car. He lowers the passenger window and speaks to one of the women, DOWELL. MOSS asks, *'How much for a fuck?'* DOWELL is not a prostitute and is in fact going out for the night with her friends. She tells MOSS to *'Drop dead!'* MOSS gets out of his car and walks up to DOWELL and says, *'C'mon, don't play hard to get. How much for a shag?'* DOWELL threatens to call the police and MOSS gets into his car and drives away.

Does MOSS commit an offence of soliciting by 'kerb-crawling' (contrary to s. 51A of the Sexual Offences Act 2003)?

A Yes, the offence is committed the moment MOSS first solicits DOWELL (when he is inside his car).
B No, the offence has not been committed unless it can be shown that the soliciting by MOSS was likely to cause nuisance or annoyance to others.
C Yes, the offence is committed but only when MOSS approaches DOWELL on foot.
D No, the offence has not been committed as DOWELL is not a prostitute.

Answer Sheet

Blackstone's Police Investigators' Mock Examination Paper 2021

72/80
71/80

Blackstone's Police Investigators' Mock Examination Paper 2021

Answer Booklet

1. Answer **B** — A sample taken from under a nail is a non-intimate sample.

   A non-intimate sample may be taken from a detainee only with their written consent or if para. 6.6 of Code D applies. Paragraph 6.6 of Code D states that a non-intimate sample may be taken from a person *without the appropriate consent* in a variety of circumstances (making answer D incorrect). These circumstances include those under para. (a) which states that a non-intimate sample can be obtained under s. 63(2A) of the Police and Criminal Evidence Act 1984 from a person who is in police detention as a consequence of being arrested for a recordable offence and who has not had a non-intimate sample of the same type and from the same part of the body taken in the course of the investigation of the offence by the police or they have had such a sample taken but it proved insufficient (this is the situation with NELHAM). No authorisation from an inspector or custody officer is required (making answers A and C incorrect).

   Investigators' Manual, para. 1.8.7.4

2. Answer **A** — The offence under s. 22 of the Theft Act 1968 is committed when a person handles goods that they *know or believe* to have been stolen. Suspecting that the property is stolen would not be enough (which eliminates the 'Yes' responses at answers C and D). The person who commits the s. 22 offence does not have to gain anything from their actions (making answer B incorrect)—in fact the retention, removal, disposal or realisation element of the offence must be done by or for the benefit of another (in this case MARLOW).

   Investigators' Manual, paras 3.7.1 to 3.7.4

3. Answer **B** — Answer C is incorrect as the School Standards and Framework Act 1998 outlaws corporal punishment in *all* British schools, including independent schools, although staff may use reasonable force in restraining violent or disruptive pupils. The Divisional Court has held that this legislation removes entirely the defence of lawful chastisement from any teacher when they are acting as such (*R (On the Application of Williamson)* v *Secretary of State for Education and Employment* [2001] EWHC Admin 960, later affirmed by the House of Lords [2005] UKHL 15). Answer A is incorrect as s. 58 of the Children Act 2004 removes the defence of lawful chastisement for parents or adults acting *in loco parentis* (meaning 'in place of the parent') where the accused person is charged with assault occasioning actual bodily harm (Offences Against the Person Act 1861, s. 47), wounding or causing grievous bodily harm (Offences Against the Person Act 1861, s. 18 or s. 20) or child cruelty (Children and Young Persons Act 1933, s. 1) to persons less than 18 years of age. However, the lawful chastisement defence

remains available for parents and adults acting *in loco parentis* charged with common assault under the Criminal Justice Act 1988, s. 39. So the defence would be available in relation to the battery against the children (making answer D incorrect). CPS charging standards state that if an injury to a child amounts to no more than reddening of the skin, and the injury is transient and trifling, a charge of common assault may be laid against the defendant for whom the lawful chastisement defence remains available. It is important to note that the law does not rule out physical chastisement by a parent etc. but that chastisement should only constitute 'mild smacking' rather than cause injuries subject to assault charges.

Investigators' Manual, para. 2.7.8

4. Answer **D** — Rape is committed when a person (A) intentionally penetrates the vagina, anus or mouth of another person (B) with his penis and B does not consent to the penetration and A does not reasonably believe B consents. A central element to the offence is the absence of consent (s. 74 of the Act) which states that a person consents if he or she agrees by choice and has the freedom and capacity to make that choice. In this situation, 'true' consent has been given so the offence has not been committed. Section 75 of the Act enables a court to presume that the victim did not consent if evidence presented in court proves that the circumstances involved any of the following: use of or fear of immediate violence against that or another person; unlawful detention; unconsciousness; inability to communicate due to physical disability; and/or substances that are capable of stupefying or overpowering (such as drugs) were non-consensually administered. It also has to be proved that the defendant knew of these circumstances and that the defendant carried out the act in question. Purely because violence was not used or threatened would not mean that a person consented to the relevant activity (answer B is incorrect). BUCKINGHAM may have lied about his wealth and the promise to marry but those lies were not about the nature or purpose of the relevant act, so answers A and C are incorrect.

Investigators' Manual, paras 4.2.1 to 4.2.6

5. Answer **A** — An offence under s. 16 of the Offences Against the Person Act 1861 is committed by a person who, without lawful excuse, makes to another a threat, *intending* that that other would fear it would be carried out, to kill that other or a third person. TAPSTER did not have the relevant intention so answer A is correct. The threat can be to kill in the future (making answer B incorrect). It does not matter if the person who would be killed does not know of the threat (making answer C incorrect). The threat can be delivered by a third party (making answer D incorrect).

Investigators' Manual, para. 2.7.16

6. Answer **B** — Section 2 of the Fraud Act 2006 states:

   (1) A person is in breach of this section if he—
      (a) dishonestly makes a false representation, and
      (b) intends, by making the representation—
         (i) to make a gain for himself or another, or
         (ii) to cause loss to another or to expose another to the risk of loss.
   (2) A representation is false if—
      (a) it is untrue or misleading, and
      (b) the person making it knows that it is, or might be, untrue or misleading.

It is a crime of *intent*, meaning that there is no need to prove that a victim was deceived or that any gain or loss actually occurred, only that the suspect intended to carry out the fraud (making answers A and D incorrect). A false representation would include a person who advertises an item for sale (including online), purporting it to be a genuine brand when he/she knows it is a fake. Even if nobody sees the ad or responds, the person has still risked causing somebody a loss—the offence is committed the moment the item is offered (making answer C incorrect and answer B correct).

Investigators' Manual, para. 3.8.4

7. Answer **D** — Intrusive surveillance is covert surveillance that is carried out in relation to anything taking place *on residential premises* or *in any private vehicle*, and that involves the presence of an individual on the premises or in the vehicle or that is carried out by means of a surveillance device. The activity that is described in this question is not taking place *on* residential premises or in a private vehicle (although the observations are taking place *from* residential premises). Therefore, this activity is not intrusive surveillance, making answers B and C incorrect. Directed surveillance is covert surveillance that is not intrusive but is carried out in relation to a specific investigation or operation in such a manner as is likely to result in the obtaining of *private information* about any person (other than by way of an immediate response to events or circumstances such that it is not reasonably practicable to seek *authorisation* under the 2000 Act). The activity described in the question is certainly directed surveillance. The Regulation of Investigatory Powers (Directed Surveillance and Covert Human Intelligence Sources) Order 2003 (SI 2003/3171), as amended, sets out the relevant roles and ranks for those who can authorise directed surveillance. In the case of the police, the relevant rank will generally be at superintendent level and above, making answer A incorrect.

Investigators' Manual, paras 1.12.4 to 1.12.4.2

8. Answer **A** — Under s. 3 of the Sexual Offences Act 2003, a person commits an offence if he intentionally touches another person (B), the touching is sexual, B does not consent to the touching and A does not reasonably believe that B consents. It does not have to involve touching the genitals (answer B is incorrect). 'Touching' includes (but is not limited to) touching with any part of the body (answer D is incorrect), with anything else or through anything else (e.g. clothing). The offence does not require that the activity is carried out for sexual gratification (answer C is incorrect).

Investigators' Manual, paras 4.3.3 to 4.3.4

9. Answer **C** — This question is a straight lift from the Manual in relation to manslaughter by unlawful act. The test case is *R v Pagett* (1983) 76 Cr App R 279 (firing a gun at police officers then holding someone else in front of you when officers return fire).

Investigators' Manual, para. 2.1.4.1

10. Answer **D** — An eye-witness may be taken to a particular neighbourhood or place to see whether they can identify the person they saw. It is not necessary for the eye-witness to be accompanied by two officers, making answer C incorrect. Where it is practicable, a record should be made of the eye-witness's description of the suspect before asking the eye-witness to make an identification in such a manner, so rather than being a bar to taking part in a 'street'

identification, the first description is a desirable element, making answer A incorrect. Care must be taken not to provide the eye-witness with any information concerning the description of the suspect (if such information is available) and not to direct the eye-witness's attention to any individual unless, taking into account all the circumstances, this cannot be avoided. However, this does not prevent an eye-witness being asked to look carefully at the people standing around at the time or to look towards a group or in a particular direction, if this is necessary to make sure the eye-witness does not overlook a possible suspect simply because they are looking in the opposite direction, making answer B incorrect. Answer D is correct as the officer has complied with the Codes of Practice (Code D, para. 3.2).

Investigators' Manual, paras 1.8.4 to 1.8.4.2

11. Answer **A** — It seems that, apart from the offences of murder, attempted murder or treason, the defence is available against any other charge (including hijacking, *R* v *Abdul-Hussain* [1999] Crim LR 570), making answers B and C incorrect. Answer D is incorrect as the defence of 'duress of circumstances' (necessity) is only available when the crime is committed in order to avoid death or serious injury—here ROSS is not committing the crime to avoid that outcome (ROSS is the victim of blackmail of course but you are not being questioned on that offence or the possible outcomes that these circumstances would have in reality—the question is asking about duress of circumstances and nothing else).

Investigators' Manual, para. 1.4.6

12. Answer **A** — PACE s. 55A allows a person who has been arrested and is in police detention to have an X-ray taken of them or an ultrasound scan to be carried out on them (or both) if:

    (a) authorised by an officer of the rank of inspector or above who has reasonable grounds for believing that the detainee:
        (i) may have swallowed a Class A drug; and
        (ii) was in possession of that Class A drug with the intention of supplying it to another or to export; and
    (b) the detainee's appropriate consent has been given in writing.

    No force can be used.

    Making A the correct answer.

Investigators' Manual, para. 1.7.25

13. Answer **B** — An offence under s. 2 of the Sexual Offences Act 2003 is committed when a person (A)—

    (a) intentionally penetrates the vagina or anus of another person (B) with a part of his body or anything else,
    (b) the penetration is sexual,
    (c) B does not consent to the penetration, and
    (d) A does not reasonably believe that B consents.

    It does not matter that the penetration in this case was using a dildo—the penetration can be with a part of the body or anything else. However, the penetration must be of the vagina or anus, not the mouth, so answer A is incorrect. The offence is first committed when WEBSTER forces the dildo into SMALL's anus (correct answer B), meaning that answers C and D are incorrect.

Investigators' Manual, para. 4.3.1

14. Answer **C** — Answer A is incorrect as land itself cannot be stolen so if, for example, a homeowner goes on holiday and her neighbour moves a fence over a little to increase the size of his garden (and hence decrease the size of hers), this would not be regarded as theft. Answer D is incorrect as it states that there are no circumstances whatsoever whereby land can be stolen when that is not the case—for example, a trustee in charge of an estate or a person with a power of attorney who sells another's land for profit could commit theft. Taking a cultivated tree without permission amounts to theft (correct answer C). Answer B is incorrect as just because the cultivated cypress tree was not taken for sale, reward or other commercial purpose does not mean the offence of theft has not been committed—the sale, reward or other commercial purpose only applies to wild plants, fruit, flowers and fungi growing wild.

Investigators' Manual, para. 3.1.6

15. Answer **D** — Section 9 of the Sexual Offences Act 2003 states:

    (1) A person aged 18 or over (A) commits an offence if—
       (a) he intentionally touches another person (B),
       (b) the touching is sexual, and
       (c) either—
          (i) B is under 16 and A does not reasonably believe that B is 16 or over, or
          (ii) B is under 13.

    So it is plain that BORMAN has committed the offence, eliminating answers A and C. The prosecution must show that the defendant intentionally touched the victim sexually and that either the victim was under 13 (in which case the offence is complete) or that the victim was under 16 and that the defendant did not reasonably believe that he/she was 16 or over, meaning that answer B is incorrect. In either case consent is irrelevant.

Investigators' Manual, para. 4.4.2

16. Answer **B** — Whether JOSSE contracts a sexually transmitted infection or not will have no impact on the consent element of the offence of rape in circumstances such as these, making answer C incorrect. Answer A is incorrect as whilst JOSSE consented to sexual intercourse, it was a 'conditional' consent. In *Assange* v *Sweden* [2001] EWHC 2489 (Admin) the Divisional Court considered the situation in which A knew B (the complainant) would only consent to sexual intercourse if he used a condom. The court rejected the view that the conclusive presumption in s. 76 of the Sexual Offences Act 2003 would apply (meaning answer D is incorrect) and concluded that the issue of consent could be determined under s. 74 rather than s. 76 and stated that it would be open to a jury to hold that if B had made it clear that she would only consent to sexual intercourse if A used a condom then there would be no consent if, without B's consent, A did not use a condom, or removed or tore the condom. A's conduct in having sexual intercourse without a condom in circumstances where B had made it clear that she would only have sexual intercourse if A did use a condom would therefore amount to an offence (correct answer B).

Investigators' Manual, paras 4.2.1 to 4.2.6

17. Answer **C** — Answer A is incorrect as the source of the intoxication can be drink or drugs. Intoxication is not a 'general defence' as such—what intoxication does is potentially remove the necessary *mens rea* required for a defendant to commit an offence. Intoxication can be divided into two categories: voluntary intoxication (you got yourself in that condition—MINCHER) and involuntary intoxication (you are not responsible for getting in that condition—DUDLEY). The distinction is important when considering whether the offence alleged is one of 'specific' or 'basic' intent. Where an offence is a specific intent offence, such as murder, defendants who were voluntarily intoxicated at the time the offence was committed may be able to show they were so intoxicated that they were incapable of forming the *mens rea* required for the offence. An individual who is voluntarily intoxicated *would not* be able to say this if accused of an offence of basic intent (MINCHER) as the courts have accepted that a defendant is still capable of forming basic intent even when completely inebriated (*DPP* v *Majewski* [1977] AC 443), making answer D incorrect. Where the offence is a basic intent offence, such as s. 47 assault, defendants who were involuntarily intoxicated (perhaps because their drink had been spiked) at the time of the offence may be able to say that they lacked the *mens rea* for that basic intent offence. So 'intoxication' is relevant as far as DUDLEY is concerned making answer B incorrect. As involuntary intoxication can be raised in answer to a charge of basic intent (s. 47 assault) answer C is correct.

Investigators' Manual, para. 1.4.3

18. Answer **B** — Section 4A of the 1997 Act prohibits a course of conduct relating to the offence of stalking involving fear of violence or serious alarm or distress. Under s. 7(3)(a) of the Act, a 'course of conduct', in the case of a single person, involves conduct on at least two occasions in relation to that person. So although the publication of a fantasy love letter is embarrassing for MASON, that is all it is (making answer A incorrect). When BAYTON sends the email to MASON stating she will kill herself if she sees him with another woman, the two-occasions element of the offence is satisfied.

There are a number of examples of 'stalking' behaviour listed at s. 2A(3) of the Act. The listed behaviours include:

- following a person;
- contacting, or attempting to contact, a person by any means;
- publishing any statement or other material (i) relating or purporting to relate to a person, or (ii) purporting to originate from a person;
- monitoring the use by a person of the internet, email or any other form of electronic communication;
- loitering in any place (whether public or private);
- interfering with any property in the possession of a person;
- watching or spying on a person.

As you can see, BAYTON's behaviour on both occasions would be considered to be 'stalking' behaviour, making answer D incorrect.

The offence under s. 4A can be committed in two ways. The first arm of the offence prohibits a course of conduct that causes the victim to fear, on at least two occasions, *that violence will be used against him/her.* MASON does not fear such violence. However, the second arm of the offence prohibits a course of conduct which causes 'serious alarm or distress' which has a 'substantial adverse effect on the day-to-day activities of the victim'. It is designed to recognise the serious impact that stalking may have on victims, even where an explicit fear of violence is not created by each incident of stalking behaviour. The phrase 'substantial adverse effect on the usual day-to-day activities' is not defined in s. 4A, and thus its construction will be a matter for the courts via judicial interpretation. However, the Home Office considers that evidence of a substantial adverse effect caused by the stalker may include:

- victims changing their routes to work, work patterns or employment;
- victims arranging for friends or family to pick up children from school (to avoid contact with the stalker);
- victims putting in place additional security measures in their home;
- victims moving home;
- physical or mental ill-health;
- victims' deterioration in performance at work due to stress;
- victims stopping or changing the way they socialise.

As BAYTON's course of conduct results in MASON suffering stress and a deterioration in his performance at work, the offence is committed by BAYTON (answer B) which makes answer C incorrect.

Investigators' Manual, para. 2.8.6.2

19. Answer **D** — It is true that any interview of a person under arrest must take place at a police station or other authorised place of detention (answer A and Code C, para. 11.1), however, there are always exceptions. Code C states that if waiting until the interview can be conducted at such a place is likely to:

    - lead to interference with or harm to evidence connected with an offence or interference with or physical harm to other people or serious loss of, or damage to property; or
    - lead to the alerting of other people suspected of having committed an offence but not yet arrested for it; or
    - hinder the recovery of property obtained in consequence of the commission of an offence;

    then an interview can go ahead. This makes answer C incorrect as it is not just harm to people that can initiate such an interview. Answer B is also incorrect as no permission from any officer is required.

    Investigators' Manual, para. 1.9.3

20. Answer **B** — The Terrorism Act 2000, s. 34(2) states:

    (2) A constable who is not of the rank required by subsection (1) may make a designation if he considers it necessary by reason of urgency.
    (3) Where a constable makes a designation in reliance on subsection (2) he shall as soon as is reasonably practicable—
        (a) make a written record of the time at which the designation was made, and
        (b) ensure that a police officer of at least the rank of superintendent is informed.

    The period of designation begins at the time the order is made and ends on the date specified in the order. The initial designation cannot extend beyond 14 days (s. 35(2)) clearly making B the correct answer.

    Investigators' Manual, para. 2.4.7.6

21. Answer **C** — In law, the offence under s. 12 (TWOC) cannot be attempted as it is a summary only offence, meaning that answer D is incorrect. A person commits an offence under s. 12 if, without having the consent of the owner or other lawful authority, he/she takes any conveyance for his/her own or another's use or, knowing that any conveyance has been taken without such authority, drives it or allows him/herself to be carried on it. This offence requires the conveyance to move therefore it does not occur until POXSON starts the vehicle and it moves 4 feet (correct answer C).

Investigators' Manual, paras 3.6.2 and 3.6.4

22. Answer **C** — The Proceeds of Crime Act 2002, s. 329 states:

    A person commits an offence if he—

    (a) acquires criminal property;
    (b) uses criminal property;
    (c) has possession of criminal property.

    An additional defence exists under s. 329(2)(c), which states that a person will not commit the offence if he acquired or used or had possession of the property for adequate consideration. The effect of the defence is that persons, such as tradesmen, who are paid for ordinary consumable goods and services in money that comes from crime, are not under any obligation to question the source of the money, making C the correct answer.

Investigators' Manual, para. 3.9.6

23. Answer **D** — The *mens rea* for the offence of assault is the intention or subjectively reckless act which caused the victim to apprehend the immediate infliction of unlawful force. However, words can also negate an assault (*Tuberville* v *Savage* (1669) 1 Mod R3). In this type of assault the defendant is making a *hypothetical* threat and is really saying 'If it weren't for the existence of certain circumstances, I would assault you'. Making D the correct option.

Investigators' Manual, para. 2.7.2.4

24. Answer **B** — The Sexual Offences Act 2003, s. 25 states:

    (1) A person (A) commits an offence if—
        (a) he intentionally touches a person (B),
        (b) the touching is sexual,
        (c) the relation of A to B is within section 27,
        (d) A knows or could reasonably be expected to know that his relation to B is of a description falling within that section, and
        (e) either—
            (i) B is under 18 and A does not reasonably believe that B is 18 or over, or
            (ii) B is under 13.

    Under s. 25 of the Sexual Offences Act 2003 there are offences that apply to blood relatives and those where certain persons have lived in the same household that are not blood relatives until the victim is 18. With these later categories, there are exceptions under s. 27 for this group. Either they were having sex before they became so related; for instance, a step-brother and step-sister who were in a sexual relationship before they became step-brother and step-sister when both 16 or over, or they are legally married in the case of Henry and Jayne, which makes B the correct answer.

Investigators' Manual, para. 4.4.11

25. Answer **B** — When a break is a short one and both the suspect and an interviewer remain in the interview room, the recording media may be stopped. There is no need to remove the recording media and when the interview recommences it shall be recorded on the same audio recording.

Investigators' Manual, para. 1.9.10.6

26. Answer **C** — Section 2(6) of the Modern Slavery Act 2015 states that a person who is a UK national (that includes a British citizen) commits an offence under this section regardless of where the arranging or facilitating takes place, meaning that answer A is incorrect. Answer D is incorrect as the exploitation can take place in any part of the world. The offence under s. 2 of the Modern Slavery Act is committed by arranging or facilitating the travel of another person ('V') with a view to V being exploited. BUCHANAN therefore commits the offence when the arrangements are made (correct answer C), meaning that answer B is incorrect.

Investigators' Manual, para. 2.10.5

27. Answer **A** — The Sexual Offences Act 2003, s. 30 states:

    (1) A person (A) commits an offence if—
        (a) he intentionally touches another person,
        (b) the touching is sexual,
        (c) B is unable to refuse because of or for a reason related to a mental disorder, and
        (d) A knows or could reasonably be expected to know that B has a mental disorder and that because of it or for a reason related to it B is likely to be unable to refuse.

    Clearly, in these circumstances TENANT was not aware of HANNAH's condition so A is the correct answer. You must also remember that it must be an intentional touching as this can be tested in this section and others within the exam.

Investigators' Manual, para. 4.5.3

28. Answer **D** — HENNIGAN is the owner of the car—it certainly belongs to him, meaning that answer C is incorrect. ORCHARD has possession of the vehicle—it belongs to him, meaning that answer A is incorrect. TREMELING has a proprietary interest in the car as parts from his garage have been used to service and repair it, meaning that answer B is incorrect and answer D is correct.

Investigators' Manual, paras 3.1.1 and 3.1.8

29. Answer **D** — Section 11 of the Fraud Act 2006 states:

    (1) A person is guilty of an offence under this section if he obtains services for himself or another—
        (a) by a dishonest act, and
        (b) in breach of subsection (2).

(2) A person obtains services in breach of this subsection if—
 (a) they are made available on the basis that payment has been, is being or will be made for or in respect of them,
 (b) he obtains them without any payment having been made for or in respect of them or without payment having been made in full, and
 (c) when he obtains them, he knows—
  (i) that they are being made available on the basis described in paragraph (a), or
  (ii) that they might be,
 but intends that payment will not be made, or will not be made in full.

The offence is committed if a person dishonestly obtains a service for another (in this case COLLIER obtains the 'service' for KNOWLE), making answer C incorrect. The term 'service' is not defined by the Act. The fact that 'service' is not defined means that in the situation where a person obtains the 'services' of a prostitute without intending to pay him/her, that person can commit an offence under s. 11 of the Fraud Act 2006, making answer A incorrect. Unlike the other Fraud Act 2006 offences, the offence under s. 11 is not a conduct crime; it is a result crime and requires the actual obtaining of the service to be complete. The offence would not be complete at point B when COLLIER lies to ORCHARD about the payment having been made—no service had been provided at that stage.

Investigators' Manual, para. 3.8.9

30. Answer **C** — The Sexual Offences Act 2003, s. 4 states:

(1) A person (A) commits an offence if—
 (a) he intentionally causes another person (B) to engage in an activity;
 (b) the activity is sexual;
 (c) B does not consent to the activity; and
 (d) A does not reasonably believe B consents.

Section 4 is committed when PARSON forces CLARK to masturbate him and forces her to prostitute herself. These are examples from the Keynote area of the Manual and show how important it is to familiarise yourself with the Keynote areas in your preparation for the exam.

Investigators' Manual, para. 4.3.5

31. Answer **C** — The Child Abduction Act 1984, s. 1 states:

(4) A person does not commit an offence under this section by taking or sending a child out of the United Kingdom without the appropriate consent if—
 (a) he is a person in whose favour there is a child arrangement order in force with respect to the child, and he takes or sends the child out of the United Kingdom for a period of less than one month; or
 (b) he is a special guardian of the child and he takes or sends the child out of the United Kingdom for a period of less than 3 months.

Therefore C is the correct answer.

Investigators' Manual, para. 2.9.2.2

32. Answer **B** — Section 2 of the Criminal Damage Act 1971 states:

A person who without lawful excuse makes to another a threat, intending that that other would fear it would be carried out,—

(a) to destroy or damage any property belonging to that other or a third person; or
(b) to destroy or damage his own property in a way which he knows is likely to endanger the life of that other or a third person;

shall be guilty of an offence.

This is all about the intention of the offender and has nothing whatsoever to do with the 'victim' of the offence. So the fact that SMITH does not believe MANNIGER is immaterial (making answer C incorrect). 'Conditional' threats are relevant to offences of assault but not to threats to commit criminal damage, making answer A incorrect. Answer D is incorrect as the threat was made to SMITH and not INCE. The offence is committed by a person (MANNIGER) who without lawful excuse makes to another (SMITH) a threat, intending that *that* other (SMITH not INCE) would fear it would be carried out. So the offence is committed because MANNIGER made the threat to SMITH (regardless of what INCE believes/fears—correct answer B).

Investigators' Manual, para. 3.10.5

33. Answer **B** — Paragraph 16.5 of Code C states that a detainee may not be interviewed about an offence after they have been charged with it, or informed that they may be prosecuted for it, unless the interview is necessary:

- to prevent or minimise harm or loss to some other person, or the public;
- to clear up an ambiguity in a previous answer or statement;
- in the interests of justice for the detainee to have put to them, and have an opportunity to comment on, information concerning the offence which has come to light since they were charged or informed that they might be prosecuted.

The fact that such an interview can take place means that answers A and C are incorrect. You would not require the authority/permission of an officer of the rank of superintendent or above to carry out such an interview, meaning that answer D is incorrect.

Investigators' Manual, para. 1.7.17

34. Answer **C** — Code B, para. 3.4 states that applications for all search warrants must be made with the written authority of an officer of at least the rank of *inspector* (although in urgent cases where such an officer is not readily available, the most senior officer on duty may authorise the application), making answer A incorrect. Answer B is incorrect as s. 16(3) of PACE states that entry and search under such a warrant must be made within *three* months from the date of its issue. If the warrant is an all premises warrant, no premises which are not specified in it may be entered and searched unless a police officer of at least the rank of *inspector* has, in writing, authorised them to be entered (s. 16(3A)) making answer D incorrect.

Investigators' Manual, para. 1.6.4

35. Answer **A** — It seems that, apart from the offence of murder, attempted murder or treason, the defence is available against any other charge (including hijacking, R v Abdul-Hussain [1999] Crim LR 570), making answers C and D incorrect.

    The 'serious injury' element relates to the thoughts of the defendant and not to the injury received by the victim, making answer B incorrect. This defence was examined by the Court of Appeal in a case where someone jumped onto the bonnet of the car that the appellant was driving (not too dissimilar from the circumstances of the question). The appellant drove for some distance with the man on the bonnet of the car, braking after a short time to go over a speed ramp. The man fell from the bonnet and the appellant drove on, running the man over and causing him grievous bodily harm. In determining whether or not the defence of 'duress of circumstances' was available, the court held that the jury must ask two questions in relation to the appellant:

    - Was he (or might he have been) impelled to act as he did because, as a result of what he reasonably believed, he had good cause to fear he would suffer death or serious injury if he did not do so?
    - If so, would a sober person of reasonable firmness and sharing the same characteristics, have responded to the situation in the way that he did?

    If each question was answered with a 'yes', the defence would be made out (R v Cairns [1999] 2 Cr App R 137).

    DRISCOLL did not fear that he would suffer death or serious injury so the defence of duress of circumstances would not be valid.

    Investigators' Manual, para. 1.4.6

36. Answer **B** — An STPO can be made and the maximum time this order can be made for is five years initially, making B the correct answer.

    Investigators' Manual, para. 2.10.7.4

37. Answer **B** — Section 12 of the Terrorism Act 2000 creates a variety of offences relating to proscribed organisations. This includes inviting support; arranging or managing (or assisting in doing so) a meeting of three or more people in public or private to support, further the activities or be addressed by a person belonging to a proscribed organisation; or addressing a meeting to encourage support or further the activities of the organisation. It does not matter that the meeting was arranged to take place in a private place (answer A is incorrect) and there is no requirement for the meeting to be for five or more people (answer C is incorrect). Simply arranging the meeting is enough (correct answer B) which means that answer D is incorrect.

    Investigators' Manual, para. 2.4.2.1

38. Answer **A** — Section 21 of the Firearms Act 1968 places restrictions on convicted persons in respect of their possession of firearms and/or ammunition.

    Any person who has been sentenced to:

    - custody for *life*, or
    - preventive detention, imprisonment, corrective training, youth custody or detention in a young offender institution for three years or more

must not, *at any time*, have a firearm or ammunition in his/her possession, i.e. a life-time ban.

So s. 21 applies to CONRAD (making answer B incorrect). It does not matter where the possession activity takes place (making answer D incorrect). The ban on possession applies to firearms and ammunition (making answer C incorrect).

Investigators' Manual, para. 2.3.13

39. Answer **C** — Section 12A of the Theft Act 1968 states:

    (1) Subject to subsection (3) below, a person is guilty of aggravated taking of a vehicle if—
        (a) he commits an offence under section 12(1) above (in this section referred to as a 'basic offence') in relation to a mechanically propelled vehicle; and
        (b) it is proved that, at any time after the vehicle was unlawfully taken (whether by him or another) and before it was recovered, the vehicle was driven, or injury or damage was caused, in one or more of the circumstances set out in paragraphs (a) to (d) of subsection (2) below.
    (2) The circumstances referred to in subsection (1)(b) above are—
        (a) that the vehicle was driven dangerously on a road or other public place;
        (b) that, owing to the driving of the vehicle, an accident occurred by which injury was caused to any person;
        (c) that, owing to the driving of the vehicle, an accident occurred by which damage was caused to any property, other than the vehicle;
        (d) that damage was caused to the vehicle.

    The first thing that is required for the offence under s. 12A to be committed is that the 'basic' offence (under s. 12 of the Theft Act 1968) must be committed. The offence under s. 12 (taking a conveyance without consent) requires the conveyance to move—starting the ignition does not accomplish that so the 'basic' offence is not committed at answer A. Additionally, none of the circumstances listed at s. 12A(2)(a) to (d) have occurred at this stage. The fact that BANSKI does not have a driving licence has no bearing on the commission of an offence under s. 12A. Driving the vehicle out of the display area would result in the commission of the s. 12 offence (TWOC) but there is still no 'aggravated' activity, meaning answer B is incorrect. The offence is *first* committed at answer C as at this time damage is caused to the vehicle (an aggravating factor under s. 12A(2)(d)). The offence is also committed at answer D but the question specifically asks when it is *first* committed.

    Investigators' Manual, para. 3.6.9

40. Answer **B** — Section 13 of the Sexual Offences Act 2003 is an offence created to cover offences 9 to 12 of the Sexual Offences Act 2003 when the offender is under the age of 18 years which lowers the sentence to the like offence of s. 9 from 14 years' imprisonment to 5 years.

    A is incorrect because s. 3 sexual touching would apply when there was no consent by SMYTH. Because SMYTH is aged between 13 years and 16 years, although having consented, it is not true consent therefore it is not s. 3. If WENTWORTH were 18 years old the offence would be s. 9 but because he is under 18 the created offence of s. 13 applies. They would both commit the offence only if they were both under the age of 16 but over the age of 13.

    Investigators' Manual, para. 4.4.6

41. Answer **D** — The disclosure provisions of the Criminal Procedure and Investigations Act 1996 set out the retention periods for case material.

    Where a person has been convicted, all material which may be relevant must be retained at least until:

    - the person is released from custody or discharged from hospital in cases where the court imposes a custodial sentence or hospital order;
    - in all other cases, for six months from the date of conviction.

    If a person is released from the custodial sentence or discharged from hospital earlier than six months from the date of conviction, material must be retained for at least six months from the date of conviction. Therefore B is incorrect as it cannot be disposed of on release, and furthermore A is incorrect in this regard and with regard to the three months served. C is incorrect not only on lengths but also the fact that custodial sentences and hospital orders do not have different rules. D is therefore correct.

    Investigators' Manual, para. 1.11.8

42. Answer **D** — Section 54A of the Police and Criminal Evidence Act 1984 (as inserted by the Anti-terrorism, Crime and Security Act 2001) provides a power to search and/or examine detained persons without their consent. This must be in order to ascertain whether the person has any mark that would tend to identify him/her as a person involved in the commission of an offence or to assist to identify him/her. Mark includes features and injuries. The search/examination is authorised by an officer of at least the rank of inspector. Authorisation may be given orally or in writing but if given orally it must be confirmed in writing as soon as possible.

    Investigators' Manual, paras 1.8.6 to 1.8.6.1

43. Answer **A** — If it appears that a person does not understand the caution, the person giving it should explain it in his/her own words.

    Investigators' Manual, para. 1.9.2

44. Answer **B** — The interviewer shall sign the label and also ask the suspect or any third party present during the interview to sign it. If the suspect or third party refuses to sign the label, an officer of at least the rank of inspector or if not available, the custody officer or, if the suspect has not been arrested, a sergeant shall be called to the interview room and asked to sign it. Making B the correct answer.

    Investigators' Manual, para. 1.9.10

45. Answer **B** — Code D deals with the process of taking footwear impressions in connection with a criminal investigation. Impressions of a person's footwear may be taken in connection with the investigation of an offence only with their consent or if para. 4.17 applies. If the person is at a police station consent must be in writing. Paragraph 4.17 states that s. 61A of PACE provides power for a police officer to take footwear impressions without consent from any person over the age of 10 years who is detained at a police station:

(a) in consequence of being arrested for a recordable offence, or if the detainee has been charged with a recordable offence, or informed they will be reported for such an offence; and
(b) the detainee has not had an impression of their footwear taken in the course of the investigation of the offence unless the previously taken impression is not complete or is not of sufficient quality to allow satisfactory analysis, comparison or matching (whether in the case in question or generally).

This makes answers A and C incorrect (as the consent of PIGDEN or FARROW is not required). It is not necessary that the footprints are taken to prove or disprove the detained person's involvement in the offence, making answer D incorrect. Paragraph 4.18 of Code D states that reasonable force may be used, if necessary, to take a footwear impression from a detainee without consent under the power in para. 4.17 (correct answer B). A record must be made as soon as possible of the reason for taking a person's footwear impressions without consent. If force is used, a record shall be made of the circumstances and those present (Code D, para. 4.20).

Investigators' Manual, para. 1.8.5.3

46. Answer **C** — The Sexual Offences Act 2003, s. 63 states:

(1) A person commits an offence if—
  (a) he is a trespasser on any premises,
  (b) he intends to commit a relevant sexual offence on the premises, and
  (c) he knows that, or is reckless as to whether, he is a trespasser.

This offence is a preparatory sexual offence of intent making A incorrect. The intent to commit a relevant sexual offence can be formed even when already on the premises as a trespasser not necessarily before entry; making D incorrect. A garden is premises for the purposes of s. 63 making B incorrect and C the correct option.

Investigators' Manual, para. 4.7.3

47. Answer **D** — Section 89 of the Police Act 1996 states:

(2) Any person who resists or wilfully obstructs a constable in the execution of his duty, or a person assisting a constable in the execution of his duty, shall be guilty of an offence.

There is no need for a physical 'obstruction' to be offered to the officer for the offence to be committed, making answer A incorrect. Answer C is incorrect as whilst obstruction can be caused by omission, this will only be where the defendant was already under some duty towards the police or the officer and that is not the case with an ordinary member of the public being asked questions by a police officer. Answer B is incorrect as refusing to answer an officer's questions is not obstruction (*Rice v Connolly* [1966] 2 QB 414). Obstruction may take many forms, e.g. deliberately providing misleading information (*Ledger* v *DPP* [1991] Crim LR 439), meaning that the correct answer is D.

Investigators' Manual, para. 2.7.15.3

48. Answer **B** —The issue of transferred *mens rea* can be important in relation to the liability of accessories (in this question POLLOCK is the principal and GUBBIN is the accessory (by counselling the assault)). If POLLOCK's intentions are to be extended to GUBBIN, it must be

shown that those intentions were either contemplated and accepted by GUBBIN at the time of the offence, or that they were 'transferred'. There is an excellent example of this in the *Investigators' Manual* which follows the storyline of this question.

EXAMPLE

A person (X) encourages another (Y) to assault Z. Y decides to attack a different person instead. X will not be liable for that assault because it was not contemplated or agreed by X. If, however, in trying to assault Z, Y happens to injure a third person inadvertently, then 'transferred *mens rea*' would result in X being liable for those injuries even though X had no wish for that person to be so injured.

So GUBBIN would not be liable for the assault injuries to EDGE (making answers C and D incorrect). GUBBIN would be liable for the assault injuries to CRANSHAW and BUTTON (correct answer B) making answer A incorrect.

Investigators' Manual, para. 1.1.12

49. Answer **D** — The Public Order Act 1986, s. 18 states:

    (1) A person who uses threatening, abusive or insulting words or behaviour, or displays any written material which is threatening, abusive or insulting is guilty of an offence if—
        (a) he intends to stir up racial hatred, or
        (b) having regard to all the circumstances racial hatred is likely to be stirred up.

    There is however, a defence under s. 18(4).

    In proceedings for an offence under this section it is a defence for the accused to prove that he was inside a dwelling and had no reason to believe that the words or behaviour used, or the written material displayed, would be heard or seen by a person outside that or any other dwelling.

    This makes D the correct answer. Sections 18 and 19 of the Public Order Act 1986 have been tested in the exam so some revision is advisable on this subject area.

    Investigators' Manual, para. 2.8.2.1

50. Answer **D** — The Criminal Attempts Act 1981 tells us that an attempt is an action that is 'more than merely preparatory' to the commission of an offence. An example of where the defendant was held to have done no more than merely preparatory acts was *R v Campbell* [1991] Crim LR 268 where the appellant armed himself with an imitation gun, approached to within a yard of a post office which he intended to rob, but never drew his weapon; it was held that there was no evidence on which a jury could properly have concluded that his acts went beyond mere preparation. That would eliminate options A, B and C leaving us with option D as the correct answer—CHUKKA has certainly gone beyond mere preparation at this point.

    Investigators' Manual, para. 1.3.4

51. Answer **D** — Robbery is committed when a person steals and immediately before or at the time of doing so, and in order to do so, they use force on any person or put or seek to put

any person in fear of being then and there subjected to force. However, there must be a theft for a robbery to occur ('and thief and steal shall be construed accordingly') which means answer B is incorrect as at that stage no theft has occurred. When force is threatened in order to steal it must be 'there and then'—at that time and at that place—so when the threat is made to shoot BEATON's wife it would not satisfy that element of the offence (although you do have an offence of blackmail at this point). But when force is used to steal, the force used does not have to be on the victim of the theft (making answer C incorrect) or at the scene of the theft (making answer A incorrect)—it could be used anywhere (correct answer D).

Investigators' Manual, para. 3.2.1

52. Answer **A** — Answer D is incorrect as, for the power under s. 32 to be lawfully used, the officer would have to have reasonable grounds for believing (not suspecting) that the arrested person may present a danger to himself or others. Answer B is incorrect as the officer has a power under s. 32(2)(ii) to search the arrested person for anything which might be evidence relating to *an offence* (not just the offence for which the person was arrested). Answer C is incorrect as PC ARROW can search in PURLEY's mouth (see s. 32(4)). Answer A is the correct answer as trespassing on land with a firearm is a *summary only* offence. Section 32(2)(b) allows an officer to enter and search any premises where the offender was when arrested or immediately before for evidence relating to the offence but only if the offence for which he/she was arrested was *indictable*.

Investigators' Manual, para. 1.6.5.2

53. Answer **A** — Section 4 of the Misuse of Drugs Act 1971 states:

    (3) Subject to section 28 of this Act, it is an offence for a person—
        (a) to supply or offer to supply a controlled drug to another in contravention of subsection (1) above; or
        (b) to be concerned in the supplying of such a drug to another in contravention of that subsection; or
        (c) to be concerned in the making to another in contravention of that subsection of an offer to supply such a drug.

    In *R v Maginnis* [1987] AC 303, the House of Lords held that 'supply' involves more than a mere transfer of physical control of the item from one person to another but includes a further concept, namely that of 'enabling the recipient to apply the thing handed over to purposes for which he desires or has a duty to apply it'. In other words, *the person to whom the drug is given must derive some benefit from being given the drug.* So the key to working out if there has been a 'supply' is to ask 'Does being given the drug benefit the person to whom the drug has been given?' If the answer is 'Yes' then the person *giving the drug* is 'supplying' it. In this question CORCORAN offers SHAW £20 to look after the cannabis—so SHAW benefits from being given the drug and therefore CORCORAN supplies it to him. When SHAW hands the cannabis back to CORCORAN, CORCORAN benefits from it as he can smoke the cannabis—therefore SHAW supplies CORCORAN.

    So at this stage CORCORAN and SHAW have committed the offence under s. 4(3) meaning that answers C and D are incorrect.

Section 4A of the Misuse of Drugs Act 1971 requires courts to treat certain conditions as 'aggravating' factors when considering the seriousness of the offence under s. 4(3) if committed by a *person aged 18 or over*. This means that s. 4A will not apply to SHAW as he is 17 years old and means that answer B is incorrect.

Investigators' Manual, paras 2.2.4.1 to 2.2.4.2

54. Answer **B** — 'Special warnings' do not apply to interviews with suspects who have not been arrested. This makes answers A, C and D incorrect.

Investigators' Manual, para. 1.9.2.5

55. Answer **C** — Section 3A(4) of the Bail Act 1976 states that where a custody officer has granted bail in criminal proceedings, he or *another custody officer* serving at the *same police station* may, at the request of the person to whom it was granted, vary the conditions of bail and in doing so he may impose conditions or more serious conditions, making answers A, B and D incorrect.

Investigators' Manual, para. 1.10.7.3

56. Answer **C** — For the s. 11 offence the offender must know or believe that the child (under 16 so answer D is incorrect) will be aware of the sexual acts in some way (e.g. seeing it live, or on a webcam or hearing it (so answer A is incorrect)), and gain some sexual gratification from the child's presumed awareness. It does not have to be carried out in the 'physical presence' of the victim so answer B is incorrect. However, the victim does not actually have to be aware of the activity (e.g. if the child does not notice).

Investigators' Manual, para. 4.4.2

57. Answer **A** — It is an offence at common law to falsely imprison another person. The elements required for this offence are the unlawful and intentional/reckless restraint of a person's freedom of movement, making answer C incorrect. Locking someone in a vehicle or keeping him/her in a particular place for however short a time may amount to false imprisonment if done unlawfully, so answer D is incorrect. Physical contact is not required between offender and victim, meaning that answer B is incorrect.

Investigators' Manual, para. 2.10.1

58. Answer **B** — Section 46 of the Children Act 1989 states:

(1) Where a constable has reasonable cause to believe that a child would otherwise be likely to suffer significant harm, he may—
    (a) remove the child to suitable accommodation and keep him there; or
    (b) take such steps as are reasonable to ensure the child's removal from any hospital, or other place, in which he is then being accommodated is prevented.

A 'child' is someone who is under 18 years old (s. 105), so CATO is classed as a 'child' and answer A is incorrect. The power under s. 46 is split into two parts:

- a power to remove a child to suitable accommodation and keep him/her there; and
- a power to take reasonable steps to *prevent* the child's removal from a hospital or other place.

If PC BUCKINGHAM has reasonable cause to believe that the child would otherwise be likely to suffer serious harm, he may take such steps as are reasonable to prevent CATO from being removed from the hospital (correct answer B). The power under s. 46 does not require the authority of an inspector (answer C is therefore incorrect). It does not allow the removal/preventing of removal of any person but the child in question, making answer D incorrect.

Investigators' Manual, para. 2.9.4

59. Answer **A** — Where a person is remanded in custody it normally means detention in prison. However, s. 128 of the Magistrates' Courts Act 1980 provides that a magistrates' court may remand a person to police custody:

- for a period not exceeding three clear days (24 hours for persons under 18 (s. 91(5) of the Legal Aid, Sentencing and Punishment of Offenders Act 2012) (s. 128(7));
- for the purpose of enquiries into offences (other than the offence for which he/she appears before the court) (s. 128(8)(a));
- as soon as the need ceases he/she must be brought back before the magistrates (s. 128(8)(b));
- the conditions of detention and periodic review apply as if the person was arrested without warrant on suspicion of having committed an offence (s. 128(8)(c) and (d)).

So FELL could be remanded in police custody for a period not exceeding three clear days and SAYER could be remanded in police custody for a period not exceeding 24 hours, meaning that answers B, C and D are incorrect.

Investigators' Manual, para. 1.10.12

60. Answer **A** — The Serious Crime Act 2007, s. 44 states:

    (1) A person commits an offence if—
        (a) he does an act capable of encouraging or assisting in the commission of an offence; and
        (b) he intends to encourage or assist its commission.
    (2) But he is not to be taken to have intended to encourage or assist the commission of an offence merely because such encouragement or assistance was a foreseeable consequence of his act.

Section 51 limits the liability of the offence by setting out in statute the exception established in the case *R v Tyrrell* [1894] 1 QB 710. Therefore a person cannot be guilty under ss. 44, 45 and 46 of this Act; that is a 'protective' offence, making A the correct answer as FIELD was encouraging an offence that is for her own protection.

Investigators' Manual, para. 1.3.2

61. Answer **C** — Under the Sexual Offences (Amendment) Act 1992, victims of most sexual offences (including rape, assault by penetration and sexual assault by touching) are entitled to anonymity throughout their lifetime.

Investigators' Manual, para. 4.1.3

62. Answer **A** — Section 9 of the Theft Act 1968 states:

    (1) A person is guilty of burglary if—

(a) he enters any building or part of a building as a trespasser and with intent to commit any such offence as is mentioned in subsection (2) below; or …
(2) The offences referred to in subsection (1)(a) above are offences of stealing anything in the building or part of a building in question, of inflicting on any person therein any grievous bodily harm and of doing unlawful damage to the building or anything therein.

It would be essential for any s. 9(1)(a) burglary that the person concerned entered as a trespasser. That is not the case for David HOWE as he is entering his own home. If FISHER is entering with David HOWE believing that David HOWE is exercising a lawful right, then FISHER cannot be a trespasser either. Add to this that neither has the intention to steal, inflict grievous bodily harm or commit criminal damage and you would not have a s. 9(1)(a) offence, meaning answer B is incorrect (if both believe there is a legal entitlement to the property then there is no dishonesty and there would be no theft element).

Section 9 of the Theft Act 1968 states:

(1) A person is guilty of burglary if—
    …
    (b) having entered any building or part of a building as a trespasser he steals or attempts to steal anything in the building or that part of it or inflicts or attempts to inflict on any person therein any grievous bodily harm.

Answer C is incorrect as David HOWE is not a trespasser. David HOWE commits theft when he takes the watch belonging to his wife (making answer D incorrect). However, where the property in question belonged to the defendant's spouse or civil partner, a prosecution for theft may only be instituted against the defendant by or with the consent of the DPP (s. 30(4)). This restriction must also apply to charges of robbery or of burglary by stealing, etc. but does not apply to other persons charged with committing the offence jointly with D; nor does it apply when the parties are separated by judicial decree or order or under no obligation to cohabit (s. 30(4)(a)).

Investigators' Manual, paras 3.4.1 to 3.5.2

63. Answer **D** — Robbery—s. 8 of the Theft Act 1968 states:

A person is guilty of robbery if he steals and immediately before or at the time of doing so, and in order to do so, he uses force on any person or puts or seeks to put any person in fear of being there and then subjected to force.

No robberies are committed. In the offence against CALDERSHAW, the prostitute, the force was not used in order to steal, and in the case of NOWAKOWSKI it was accidental application of force which also does not constitute an offence of robbery.

Investigators' Manual, para. 3.2.1

64. Answer **D** — Section 54B of the Police and Criminal Evidence Act 1984 states:

(1) A constable may search at any time—
    (a) any person who is at a police station to answer to live link bail; and
    (b) any article in the possession of such a person.

(2) If the constable reasonably believes a thing in the possession of the person ought to be seized on any of the grounds mentioned in subsection (3), the constable may seize and retain it or cause it to be seized and retained.

(3) The grounds are that the thing—
   (a) may jeopardise the maintenance of order in the police station;
   (b) may put the safety of any person in the police station at risk; or
   (c) may be evidence of, or in relation to, an offence.

(4) The constable may record or cause to be recorded all or any of the things seized and retained pursuant to subsection (2).

(5) An intimate search may not be carried out under this section.

(6) The constable carrying out a search under subsection (1) must be of the same sex as the person being searched.

Designated detention officers, as well as constables, can use the power. So although the power is available to ORWELL (making answer B incorrect), she cannot search CRABTREE as the searching officer and person searched have to be of the same sex (making answer A incorrect). Answer C is incorrect as s. 54B(3) provides three reasons why property might be seized by the searching officer. Answer D is correct as PC SAMUEL is the only officer who can search CRABTREE and articles in his possession. Section 46A(1ZB) provides a constable with a power of arrest for defendants who attend the police station to answer live link bail but refuse to be searched under s. 54B.

Investigators' Manual, para. 1.10.9.1

65. Answer **B** — Group identifications may take place either with the suspect's consent and cooperation or covertly without their consent, making answer A incorrect. Answer C is incorrect as group identifications can involve stationary or moving groups. If it is practicable, then the group identification process will be video recorded but this might not be possible (making answer D incorrect). Group identifications should only take place in police stations for reasons of safety, security or because it is not practicable to hold them elsewhere (correct answer B).

Investigators' Manual, para. 1.8.10

66. Answer **D** — Section 18 of the Police and Criminal Evidence Act 1984 states:

(1) Subject to the following provisions of this section, a constable may enter and search any premises occupied or controlled by a person who is under arrest for an indictable offence, if he has reasonable grounds for *suspecting* that there is on the premises evidence, other than items subject to legal privilege, that relates—
   (a) to that offence; or
   (b) to some other indictable offence which is connected with or similar to that offence.

(2) A constable may seize and retain anything for which he may search under subsection (1) above.

(3) The power to search conferred by subsection (1) above is only a power to search to the extent that is reasonably required for the purpose of discovering such evidence.

(4) Subject to subsection (5) below, the powers conferred by this section may not be exercised unless an officer of the rank of inspector or above has *authorised them in writing*.

The search takes place if the officer has reasonable grounds for suspecting (not believing), eliminating answers B and C. An inspector must provide his/her written authorisation, making answer A incorrect.

Investigators' Manual, para. 1.6.5.3

67. Answer **B** — Actions by the victim will sometimes be significant in the chain of causation, such as where a victim of a sexual assault was injured when jumping from her assailant's car (*R v Roberts* (1971) 56 Cr App R 95). Where such actions take place, the victim's behaviour *will not* necessarily be regarded as introducing a new intervening act. If the victim's actions are those which might reasonably be anticipated from any victim in such a situation, there will be no new and intervening act and the defendant will be responsible for the consequences flowing from them, meaning that answers A, C and D incorrect.

Investigators' Manual, para. 1.2.6

68. Answer **C** — Section 4 of the Sexual Offences Act 2003 (causing sexual activity without consent) states:

    (1) A person (A) commits an offence if—
        (a) he intentionally causes another (B) to engage in an activity,
        (b) the activity is sexual,
        (c) B does not consent to engaging in the activity, and
        (d) A does not reasonably believe that B consents.

    There is no need to prove sexual gratification, albeit that it may be the case, making answer B incorrect. WEST does not commit any offences as he was unlawfully detained at the time of the offence (evidential presumption under s. 75 of the Act). Therefore C is the correct answer.

Investigators' Manual, para. 4.3.5

69. Answer **D** — The Malicious Communications Act 1988, s. 1 states:

    (1) Any person who sends to another person—
        (a) a letter, electronic communication or article of any description which conveys—
            (i) a message which is indecent or grossly offensive;
            (ii) a threat; or
            (iii) information that is false and known or believed to be false by the sender; or
        (b) any article or electronic communication which is, in whole or part, of an indecent or grossly offensive nature.

    'Any article' includes dog faeces. This topic does crop up in the NIE so it is worth in your revision taking time to look at it. Note also the defences para. 2.5.4.1—they are very similar to blackmail defences.

Investigators' Manual, para. 2.5.4

70. Answer **D** — A defendant cannot be convicted of statutory conspiracy if the only other party to the agreement is:

    • his/her spouse or civil partner;

- a person under 10 years of age;
- the intended victim (s. 2(2) of the Criminal Law Act 1977). You can conspire to commit offences that are indictable only, triable either way or summary only, making answer A incorrect. Answer B is incorrect as although there must be a 'meeting of minds' for a conspiracy to be committed, the whole purpose of the offence is to catch behaviour leading up to the commission of the offence. Any failure to bring about the end result or abandoning of the agreement will not prevent the offence being committed. The fact that the commission of the offence is impossible as the victim is in Poland will not prevent the offence being committed (s. 1(1)(b)), making answer C incorrect.

Investigators' Manual, para. 1.3.3.1

71. Answer **A** — Robbery is committed when a person steals and immediately before or at the time of doing so, and in order to do so, they use force on any person or put or seek to put any person in fear of being then and there subjected to force. However, there must be a theft for a robbery to occur ('and thief and steal shall be construed accordingly'). If there is no theft, then there is no robbery. Here there is no theft because PUGH honestly believes that he has a lawful right to deprive CANNON of the property. The circumstances of the question are very similar to the case of *R v Robinson* [1977] Crim LR 173, where D, who was owed £7 by P's wife, approached P, brandishing a knife. A fight followed, during which P dropped a £5 note. D picked it up and demanded the remaining £2 owed to him. Allowing D's appeal against a conviction for robbery, the Court of Appeal held that the prosecution had to prove that D was guilty of theft, and that he would not be (under s. 2(1)(a) of the Theft Act 1968) if he believed that he had a right in law to deprive P of the money, even though he knew that he was not entitled to use the knife to get it, i.e. there was no dishonesty. The fact that PUGH knows the means he is using are wrong does not alter the dishonesty element.

Investigators' Manual, para. 3.2.1

72. Answer **C** — The Police and Criminal Evidence Act 1984, s. 18(1) states:

A constable may enter and search any premises **occupied** or **controlled** by a person who is under arrest for an indictable offence, if he has reasonable grounds for suspecting that there is on the premises evidence, other than items subject to legal privilege that relates—

(a) to that offence; or
(b) to some other indictable offence which is connected with or similar to that offence.

I have highlighted 'occupied or controlled' as many persons believe that it states 'owns'. Reasonable suspicion that someone occupies or controls premises is not sufficient, making C the correct option.

Investigators' Manual, para. 1.6.5.3

73. Answer **B** — Answer A is incorrect as the pain-killing drug is a form of property (*R v Bevans* (1987) 87 Cr App R 64). Blackmail is, essentially, an unwarranted demand with menaces, so answer C is incorrect as it does not matter that the menaces of criminal damage were not going to take place 'there and then' (words relevant to robbery and not blackmail). The offence of blackmail is complete at the moment the unwarranted demand with menaces is made and a

transfer of property does not need to take place for the offence to be complete, meaning that answer D is incorrect.

Investigators' Manual, paras 3.3.1 to 3.3.4

74. Answer **D** — Section 89(1) of the Police Act 1996 states:

    (1) Any person who assaults a constable in the execution of his duty, or a person assisting a constable in the execution of his duty, shall be guilty of an offence.

    This offence requires that the officer was acting in the execution of his/her duty when assaulted. If this is not proved, then part of the *actus reus* will be missing. Even a minor, technical and inadvertent act of unlawfulness on the part of the officer will mean that he/she cannot have been acting in the lawful execution of his/her duty. Any action amounting to assault, battery, unlawful arrest or trespass to property takes the officer outside the course of his/her duty (*Davis* v *Lisle* [1936] 2 KB 434). So PC VERRIN would not be acting in the execution of his duty and would not be protected by the law, making answer B incorrect. However, if a prisoner is arrested and brought before a custody officer, that officer is entitled to assume that the arrest has been lawful. Therefore, if the prisoner goes on to assault the custody officer, that assault will be an offence under s. 89(1) even if the original arrest turns out to have been unlawful (*DPP* v *L* [1999] Crim LR 752). This means that answer A is incorrect. The fact that the injuries received by PS BLACKBURN are of a minor nature does not have any bearing on the matter, making answer C incorrect. So the offence has been committed, but only against PS BLACKBURN (correct answer D).

    Investigators' Manual, para. 2.7.15.2

75. Answer **D** — The Sexual Offences Act 2003, s. 12 states:

    (1) A person aged 18 or over (A) commits an offence if—
       (a) for the purpose of obtaining sexual gratification, he intentionally causes another person (B) to watch a third person engaging in an activity, or to look at an image of any person engaging in an activity,
       (b) the activity is sexual, and
       (c) either—
           (i) B is under 16 and A does not reasonably believe B is 16 or over, or
           (ii) B is under 13.

    The issue here is whether NELSON committed the offence and if so at what point was it *first* committed. He knows her to be under 16 and the showing of the images and pictures was for sexual gratification. He can commit the offence by achieving sexual gratification from her watching of the images but, in this question, this was not the case. His motive was to lower the victim's inhibitions. Therefore he commits the offence when he first shows the first image. Image includes a moving or still image and includes an image produced by any means and, where the context permits, a three-dimensional image and it also includes an image of an imaginary person. It does not follow that the sexual gratification has to be immediate, i.e. simultaneous, contemporaneous or synchronised, it can be to put the child in the frame of mind for future sexual abuse (*R* v *Abdullahi* [2006] EWCA Crim 2060), making D the correct answer.

    Investigators' Manual, para. 4.4.5

76. Answer **C** — The minimum period a travel restriction order can run for is two years, making answer A incorrect. There is no maximum period the order can run for making answer B incorrect. Answers A and B are further incorrect as they state that a travel restriction order could be made in these circumstances when that is not the case. Such an order can only be made when the court has convicted a person of a drug trafficking offence (and production of a controlled drug under s. 4(2) of the Misuse of Drugs Act 1971 is a 'drug trafficking offence', making answer D incorrect) and it has determined that a sentence of four years or more is appropriate—as CAFFERATTA has been sentenced to a period of imprisonment of three years, the order could not be made (correct answer C).

Investigators' Manual, para. 2.2.16

77. Answer **B** — There are two forms of burglary—s. 9(1)(a) and s. 9(1)(b). The Theft Act 1968, s. 9 states:

    (1) A person is guilty of burglary if—
        (a) he enters any building or part of a building as a trespasser and with intent to commit any such offence as is mentioned in subsection (2) below; or...
    (2) The offences referred to in subsection (1)(a) above are offences of stealing anything in the building or part of a building in question, of inflicting on any person therein any grievous bodily harm and of doing unlawful damage to the building or anything therein.

    The s. 9(1)(a) offence is committed at one point only—the point of entry. The necessary intention must be in the mind of the defendant at that time and at no stage does BARKER ever 'enter' with intent so there is no offence under s. 9(1)(a) to consider at any stage.

    The Theft Act 1968, s. 9 states:

    (1) A person is guilty of burglary if—
        (b) having entered any building or part of a building as a trespasser he steals or attempts to steal anything in the building or that part of it or inflicts or attempts to inflict on any person therein any grievous bodily harm.

    BARKER has entered the warehouse as a trespasser when he breaks in looking for shelter but when he turns on the electric fire to warm himself up this is not 'stealing' as electricity is not 'property' for the purposes of the offence of theft, so no burglary is committed at point A. However, when he steals the £30 cash he does commit a s. 9(1)(b) offence (answer B is the correct answer as the question asks when is a burglary first committed). There is no burglary at point C (this is criminal damage)—a further burglary under s. 9(1)(b) is committed when BARKER steals the batteries (point D).

    Investigators' Manual, paras 3.4.1 to 3.4.5

78. Answer **B** — There are a number of offences that can be racially or religiously aggravated under the Crime and Disorder Act 1998 and criminal damage (under s. 1(1) of the Criminal Damage Act 1971) is one of the 'trigger' offences, making answer C incorrect. In the context of criminal damage, the Divisional Court has confirmed that the relevant hostility can be demonstrated even if the victim (JANKOWSKI) is no longer present or is not present (*Parry* v *DPP* [2004] EWHC 3112 (Admin)), making answer A incorrect. Section 28(1)(6) clearly states that 'racial group' means a group of persons defined by reference to race, colour, nationality (including citizenship) or ethnic or national origins, so the words sprayed on the car referring to

JANKOWSKI being Polish would certainly be covered. In *DPP* v *M* [2004] EWHC 1453 (Admin) a juvenile used the words 'bloody foreigners' immediately before smashing the window of a kebab shop. The Divisional Court held that this was capable of amounting to an expression of hostility based on a person's membership or presumed membership of a racial group for the purposes of s. 28(1)(a) of the Crime and Disorder Act 1998, meaning that answer D is incorrect.

Investigators' Manual, paras 2.6.1 to 2.6.10

79. Answer **A** — The question of admissibility is to be decided by a judge in all cases (making answer B incorrect). Answer C is incorrect as there are a variety of reasons why evidence can be excluded including the incompetence of a witness. Answer D is incorrect as evidence can be excluded under common law as well as elements of PACE 1984.

Investigators' Manual, paras 1.5.1 to 1.5.2.2

80. Answer **A** — Section 51A(1) of the Sexual Offences Act 2003 states that it is an offence for a person in a street or public place to solicit another (B) for the purpose of obtaining B's sexual services as a prostitute. The fact that the person solicited is not a prostitute is irrelevant, making answer D incorrect. Section 51A(2) states that the reference to a person in a street or public place includes a person in a vehicle in a street or public place. As 'kerb-crawling' or soliciting is punishable on the *first occasion* the activity takes place, this would mean that the offence is committed when MOSS solicits DOWELL when he (MOSS) is inside his car (correct answer A) and that makes answer C incorrect. In the case of 'kerb-crawling', there is no requirement for the soliciting to be shown to be likely to cause nuisance or annoyance to others, meaning that answer B is incorrect.

Investigators' Manual, para. 4.6.6